The Robin Takes 5 Cookbook for Busy Families

OTHER BOOKS BY ROBIN MILLER

Robin Takes 5

Robin Rescues Dinner

Quick Fix Meals

Robin to the Rescue

The Newlywed Cookbook

Picnics

The Daily Soup Cookbook

Cooking for Healthy Living (with Jane Fonda)

Verdure

The Robin Takes 5

Cookbook for

Busy Families

Over 200 Recipes with 5 Ingredients or Less for Breakfasts, School Lunches, After-School Snacks, Family Dinners, and Desserts

Robin Miller

Illustrations by Ms. Smith's third-grade class, Ms. Rabe's fourth-grade class, and Mr. Ney's fifth-grade class at Red Field Elementary

**Andrews McMeel
Publishing, LLC**
Kansas City • Sydney • London

Andrews McMeel Publishing, LLC
an Andrews McMeel Universal company
1130 Walnut Street, Kansas City, Missouri 64106

www.andrewsmcmeel.com

13 14 15 16 17 RR2 10 9 8 7 6 5 4 3 2 1

ISBN: 978-1-4494-3688-9

Library of Congress Control Number: 2013932518

Illustrations: Chloe, Cade, Cara, Tamar, Eli, Jasmine, Sicily, Kyle, and Luke

www.robinrescuesdinner.com

ATTENTION: SCHOOLS AND BUSINESSES

Andrews McMeel books are available at quantity discounts with bulk purchase for educational, business, or sales promotional use. For information, please e-mail the Andrews McMeel Special Sales Department: specialsales@amuniversal.com

This book is dedicated to *my* busy family:
Thanks for giving me inspiration
every waking moment of the day—
and for sometimes keeping me awake at night!

Contents

Acknowledgments

I would be remiss if I didn't thank *all* busy families—you consistently motivate me to create deliciously easy meals that are suitable for the entire family. Thanks for tracking me down on the soccer field, on the flag football sidelines, and in the grocery store aisles to get my advice. You keep me focused on the reality that we *all* need strategies for getting healthy and delectable dishes on the table and into lunch boxes day after day.

My busy family is no exception. Kyle and Luke, thanks for inspiring me to craft new breakfast creations most mornings and for gobbling down your school lunch every day. I have such fun making innovative meals for you (and inserting little surprises into your lunch boxes). You have my permission to keep me busy anytime you want.

Bonnie Tandy Leblang, thanks, yet again, for handling all the business affairs involved in a new book deal. Most of the work is "behind the scenes," but I know you're there. Kirsty Melville, president and publisher at Andrews McMeel, thanks for going another round! I had a lot of fun putting the "family" spin on my Take 5 concept. Jean Lucas, my editor, we did it again! And because this is our second book together, I think we had the perfect stride the entire time. Two hands, left and right, that always knew what the other was doing. Once again, thanks for including me in every detail—right down to the color of the wrap on the cover!

Bri Holloway, thanks for the fun and lively photography on the cover. You were such a great sport when the boys were running all over the place (instead of standing still for the shot)! You truly captured the spirit of my family.

Julie Barnes, I am so thrilled that you handled the design of this book. I adore it! This new collection of recipes is a joy to page through and its whimsy highlights the way I feel about cooking for my family every day.

Dave Shaw, production editor, thank you for your obvious efforts. This book has such a positive vibe and I am eager to share it with the masses! Thanks for getting it out the door in perfect style.

Have you noticed the amazing artwork throughout the book? Bet you think it's from a professional illustrator, right? Actually, the illustrations were created by several wonderful children at my boys' elementary school. Mr. Ney, Ms. Rabe, and Ms. Smith, thanks for sharing your classrooms and students with me. It was incredibly heartwarming how seriously they took the task when I asked for a few fun illustrations for "my new cookbook." The boys and girls worked *so hard,* I had goose bumps for days. Still do. *Everyone* did an incredible job, but I want to give extra-special thanks to those who did *more* art when I asked for it: Chloe, Cate, Cara, Tamar, Eli, Jasmine, and Sicily. And of course, Kyle and Luke, thank you for adding *your* designs to this amazing piece of work. Adding authentic children's art to this cookbook was not only gratifying, it gave every page the "warm and fuzzy" feel I was going for.

Introduction

Welcome, busy families! Feast your eyes (and stomach) on my latest compilation of *Take 5* recipes. I wrote this cookbook exclusively for all of us who struggle, daily, to come up with delectable yet nutritious family-friendly dishes—from breakfast to school lunch to after-school snacks to the evening meal. And I mean "us" because I face the same mealtime dilemmas, from dawn until dusk, as I strive to put fabulous fare on the table and into the lunch box. Like you, my kids and husband keep me incredibly busy; plus I'm a nutritionist, cookbook author, and TV personality. Thankfully, I have more than twenty years of recipe testing and food writing experience and have discovered the secret to creating gourmet meals and snacks with few ingredients in minimal time. By sharing my secrets in *The Robin Takes 5 Cookbook for Busy Families*, I can quench your insatiable appetite for quick and delicious food for the entire brood.

Imagine your day like this: a nourishing breakfast of Buttermilk Flapjacks with Bacon (page 13) or Huevos Rancheros on English Muffins (page 7). Or why not let the kids enjoy the Almond Coffee Cake (page 18) while you pack Chicken Caesar Pita Pockets (page 22) in their lunch boxes and spoon Lemony Sweet Pea Risotto (page 45) or Quinoa Salad with Black Beans, Corn & Cilantro (page 46) into a container for *you*? Afternoon snacks are a breeze with Roasted Corn Guacamole with Baked Tortilla Chips (page 61) and Warm Spinach Dip with Sun-Dried Tomatoes & Pepper Jack (page 62). For dinner, wow the crowd with Toasted Tortellini with Bread Crumbs & Tomato Sauce (page 75), Turkey Meatball Sliders (page 110), or Cheddar Fondue with Shrimp & Apples (page 113). Think you don't have time for dessert? There's always time for White Chocolate Truffles with Raspberry Sauce (page 199) or Crispy Sugared Wonton Ice-Cream Sandwiches (page 206). The biggest secret of all? Each recipe is ready in a flash with five ingredients or less.

My recipes are unique and unlike other so-called "family" meals because they are truly kid-friendly. Each recipe contains at least one ingredient we know kids like. You know your family, so you might choose something with a sweet element, such as a fruit-based glaze, colorful salsa, or syrupy sauce. Or maybe a savory ingredient is more appropriate, so you may choose tangy cheese and salty ham and nestle them on top of one of my pizzas. The result is a dish all family members will adore. And I went beyond the traditional cookbook because *The Robin Takes 5 Cookbook for Busy Families* features easy recipes for breakfast (at home and on the go), lunch (for school and work), and after-school snacks. I even added a bunch of slow cooker meals because I realize the appliance is a staple in many homes. In every case, from snacks to entire meals, the food is simple to prepare yet boasts foodie flavors with just five ingredients or less. And I have no tricks up my sleeve. The only staples I expect you to have (and that I don't count in the five ingredients) are olive oil, canola oil, cooking spray, salt, and freshly ground black pepper. Everything else is considered to be one of the five ingredients.

To make the cookbook even more user-friendly, I added helpful icons on every page, symbols that highlight recipes that you can Make Ahead, those that are Fun Food for kids, Finicky Friendly, Gluten-Free, ideal for Birthday Parties, as well as those that are excellent for doubling and tripling for future meals and snacks (Make a Big Batch).

I realize that creating "epi-curious" food for the whole family—quickly and easily—is just as important at 7:00 AM as it is at 7:00 PM. So, from morning until night, I've got you covered with an assortment of scrumptious selections. You'll soon discover that *The Robin Takes 5 Cookbook for Busy Families* is a book that will forever live on your kitchen counter.

A Guide to the Icons

 MAKE AHEAD: Recipes that can be made or assembled in advance and refrigerated or frozen.

 MAKE A BIG BATCH: Salsas, sauces, snack mixes, casseroles, main dishes, and more. So delicious, you'll want to stockpile. Great to have on hand for busy days and weeks.

 FUN FOOD: Dishes that are presented with a bit more styling (such as green angel hair pasta with black olive "eyes," a sour cream "spider-web" on guacamole, and more) and those that become handheld or finger-food feasts. Dishes the kids and adults will all love.

 GLUTEN-FREE: Gluten-free dishes or those that can easily be trans-formed into a gluten-free meal.

 FINICKY FRIENDLY: This icon works two ways. First, it highlights ingre-dients (spicy, zesty, tart, herbal, unfamiliar) that may be eliminated or substituted with another ingredient. Second, it points out ingredients that most kids like, meaning that the dish can please every palate in the family.

 BIRTHDAY PARTY: Recipes that are ideal for birthday parties and other celebrations with kids *and* adults.

French Toast Sticks with Maple & Cinnamon

Cheesy Egg Wraps with Ham

Broccoli & Cheese Quiche

Deviled Eggs with Smoked Paprika

Baked Cheddar Omelet with Turkey Sausage & Tomatoes

Huevos Rancheros on English Muffins

Smoked Turkey, Egg & Swiss Pockets

Egg Salad with Roasted Red Peppers on Toasted Mini Bagels

One-Egg Western Omelet

Curried Potato "Chips" with Over-Medium Eggs

Breakfast Pizza with Ricotta & Canadian Bacon

Buttermilk Flapjacks with Bacon

Mini Blueberry Pancakes

Apple Cinnamon Pancakes

Pumpernickel Squares with Vegetable Cream Cheese

Cinnamon Rolls with Brown Sugar & Walnuts

Almond Coffee Cake

Overnight Vanilla Bread Pudding

CHAPTER 1

Breakfast on the Fly

French Toast Sticks with Maple & Cinnamon

Serves 4 ■ Prep time: 15 minutes ■ Cooking time: 4 to 6 minutes

This homemade breakfast is much healthier than the processed frozen variety. Plus, you can use your favorite bread, including gluten-free varieties; cinnamon-raisin bread is great, too. The egg mixture can be made up to 24 hours in advance and refrigerated until you're ready to make the French toast. You can also soak the bread in the egg mixture for up to 12 hours (prep the night before and breakfast will be a snap).

1 cup low-fat (1%) milk or vanilla soy milk

2 large eggs

2 tablespoons pure maple syrup, plus more as desired for dipping

½ teaspoon ground cinnamon

8 slices whole wheat bread

Cooking spray

Nutrients per serving:

Calories: 232

Fat: 5g

Saturated Fat: 1.5g

Cholesterol: 93mg

Carbohydrate: 34g

Protein: 13g

Fiber: 4g

Sodium: 336mg

In a large shallow dish, whisk together the milk, eggs, maple syrup, and cinnamon. Add the bread slices, flip to coat both sides of the bread, and let stand for 10 minutes to allow the bread to soak up the milk mixture (you may let the bread soak for up to 12 hours, refrigerated).

Coat a large griddle or skillet with cooking spray and preheat over medium-high heat. Add the bread slices and cook for 2 to 3 minutes per side, until the eggs are cooked. Cut each bread slice into 4 strips and serve with additional maple syrup, if desired.

Cheesy Egg Wraps with Ham

Serves 4 ■ Prep time: 5 minutes ■ Cooking time: 5 minutes

Nutrients per serving:
Calories: 269
Fat: 12g
Saturated Fat: 5g
Cholesterol: 210mg
Carbohydrate: 19g
Protein: 17g
Fiber: 1g
Sodium: 599mg

I make these wraps all the time for my boys before school (they're super easy to eat in the car). Since my older son wakes up before my younger one, I often make one at a time (instead of four, as directed below). He also likes a little salsa nestled between the layers of ham and egg. When cooking just one egg, use your smallest skillet to create the egg "pancake" that is rolled into the tortilla. Feel free to substitute smoked turkey for the ham, or leave the meat out altogether.

4 fajita-size flour tortillas (regular or whole wheat)

½ cup shredded sharp cheddar cheese

8 thin slices smoked or baked ham (such as deli-style ham; about 4 ounces)

Cooking spray

4 large eggs

¼ teaspoon salt

¼ teaspoon freshly ground black pepper

Arrange the tortillas on a flat surface. Top each tortilla with 2 tablespoons of the cheddar cheese and 2 slices of the ham, spreading the filling to within ½ inch of the edges.

Coat a large skillet with cooking spray and preheat over medium-high heat. Whisk together the eggs, salt, and pepper and add the mixture to the hot pan. Cook, without stirring, until the bottom is set, 1 to 2 minutes. Using a spatula, flip the eggs (as if flipping a pancake). Cook for 30 more seconds, or until the egg "pancake" is cooked through. Divide each egg into 4 equal pieces, place each piece on a prepared tortilla, and roll up.

Broccoli & Cheese Quiche

Serves 8 ■ Prep time: 10 minutes ■ Cooking time: 30 to 40 minutes
Rest time: 10 minutes

Kids love to eat pie-shaped things, and this is an excellent way to provide a wholesome, fun meal in one shot. Plus, because the quiche can be assembled and baked up to 24 hours in advance, it's an excellent choice for jam-packed mornings when there's no time to cook. Individual wedges can be quickly and easily reheated in the microwave (for about 30 seconds). If you and your kids prefer spinach over broccoli, substitute one 10-ounce package of thawed frozen chopped spinach. Just make sure the spinach is well drained or the filling will be watery.

Nutrients per serving:
Calories: 258
Fat: 16g
Saturated Fat: 8g
Cholesterol: 97mg
Carbohydrate: 18g
Protein: 10g
Fiber: 1g
Sodium: 366mg

1 (9-inch) refrigerated piecrust
2 cups fresh or thawed frozen broccoli florets
1 cup shredded Gruyère or Swiss cheese
8 ounces light vegetable cream cheese, softened
3 large eggs plus 2 large egg whites
¼ teaspoon salt
¼ teaspoon freshly ground black pepper

Preheat the oven to 375°F.

Press the piecrust into the bottom and up the sides of a 9-inch pie plate.

Blanch the broccoli in a small pot of boiling water for 30 seconds (or steam in the microwave for 1 minute). Drain and arrange the broccoli in the bottom of the piecrust. Spread the shredded cheese over the broccoli.

Whisk together the cream cheese, eggs, egg whites, salt, and pepper. Pour the mixture over the broccoli and cheese. Bake for 30 to 40 minutes, until the crust is golden brown and the filling is set. Let the quiche stand for 10 minutes before slicing into wedges.

Deviled Eggs with Smoked Paprika

Serves 8 ■ Prep time: 15 to 20 minutes

Make these eggs fun by creating "faces" on top with pieces of olives, pimentos, bell peppers, or tomatoes. If you have a picky eater who doesn't like chives, simply leave them off the deviled eggs, or top the eggs with thinly sliced pimento-stuffed green olives.

These can be assembled up to 24 hours in advance. Keep them refrigerated until ready to serve. You may also boil the eggs up to 3 days in advance and refrigerate until ready to peel and proceed with the recipe.

Nutrients per serving:
Calories: 75
Fat: 4g
Saturated Fat: 1g
Cholesterol: 180mg
Carbohydrate: 1g
Protein: 6g
Fiber: <1g
Sodium: 140mg

8 large eggs
¼ cup light mayonnaise
1 teaspoon Dijon mustard
½ teaspoon smoked paprika
¼ teaspoon salt
¼ teaspoon freshly ground black pepper
2 tablespoons chopped fresh chives

Place the eggs in a large saucepan and pour over enough cold water to cover the eggs by about 2 inches. Set the pan over high heat and bring to a boil. Boil for 12 minutes. Drain and immediately plunge the eggs into ice-cold water.

When cool enough to handle, remove the shells from the eggs and halve lengthwise. Scoop out the yolks and transfer them to a medium bowl. Add the mayonnaise, mustard, smoked paprika, salt, and pepper and mix until smooth and blended. Spoon the yolk mixture into each egg white half and top with the chives.

Baked Cheddar Omelet with Turkey Sausage & Tomatoes

Serves 4 ■ Prep time: 15 minutes ■ Cooking time: 5 to 10 minutes

Nutrients per serving:
Calories: 293
Fat: 17g
Saturated Fat: 5g
Cholesterol: 400mg
Carbohydrate: 8g
Protein: 24g
Fiber: 1g
Sodium: 609mg

I love this recipe because it's an easy, one-pan dish that starts on the stove and finishes in the oven (giving you a few minutes to do other things). When I make it, my kids always say, "Mom, I hope you put this recipe in your cookbook." Plus, you can plan ahead and assemble and bake the omelet up to 24 hours before serving. Individual portions can be quickly and easily reheated in the microwave for 30 to 45 seconds. For a gluten-free breakfast, read the label on the sausage to make sure it's gluten-free. This recipe makes a fairly large omelet, so if you have small people in the house, you might get six servings out of it.

Cooking spray
8 ounces sweet or hot Italian turkey sausage, casing removed
1 (14-ounce) can diced fire-roasted tomatoes, drained
¼ cup chopped fresh basil
8 large eggs, lightly beaten
½ cup shredded sharp cheddar cheese

Preheat the oven to 375°F.

Coat a large ovenproof skillet with cooking spray and preheat over medium-high heat. Add the sausage and cook for 5 to 7 minutes, until the sausage is cooked through, breaking up the meat as it cooks. Add the tomatoes and basil and cook for 2 minutes, or until the mixture simmers and the liquid is absorbed. Add the eggs and cook without stirring for 2 to 3 minutes, until the bottom is set. Top the eggs with the cheese.

Transfer the skillet to the oven and bake for 5 to 10 minutes, until the egg mixture is completely set and the top is golden brown.

Huevos Rancheros on English Muffins

Serves 4 ■ Prep time: 10 to 15 minutes

Huevos rancheros is a classic Mexican dish that features fried eggs served on top of a tomato-chile sauce and lightly fried corn tortillas. Mexican rice, refried beans, and avocado are often served on the side. Clearly it's too much work for a school morning! I found a way to enjoy the same flavors in a fraction of the time (plus I eliminated much of the unnecessary fat). To make the dish gluten-free, use your favorite gluten-free English muffin. And for finicky eaters, use your favorite pizza or pasta sauce instead of salsa.

Nutrients per serving:
Calories: 224
Fat: 9g
Saturated Fat: 4g
Cholesterol: 193mg
Carbohydrate: 22g
Protein: 14g
Fiber: 4g
Sodium: 549mg

1 (14-ounce) can diced fire-roasted tomatoes, undrained
½ cup prepared salsa of your choice
4 large eggs
½ cup shredded Monterey Jack cheese
2 whole wheat English muffins, halved, lightly toasted

Combine the diced tomatoes and salsa in a large skillet and set the pan over medium-high heat. Bring the mixture to a simmer. Crack the eggs, one at a time, and gently drop the eggs onto the simmering tomato mixture. Simmer for 3 to 5 minutes, until the eggs are almost cooked through, spooning the simmering tomato mixture over the eggs to cook the top. Sprinkle the cheese over the eggs and simmer for 1 minute, or until the cheese melts.

Arrange the English muffin halves on plates. Spoon the tomato mixture and eggs onto the English muffins.

Smoked Turkey, Egg & Swiss Pockets

Serves 4 ■ Prep time: 10 to 15 minutes

Nutrients per serving:
Calories: 199
Fat: 7g
Saturated Fat: 2.5g
Cholesterol: 203mg
Carbohydrate: 13g
Protein: 21g
Fiber: 1g
Sodium: 486mg

These pockets are great for breakfast on the go, whether you're on the way to the bus stop or jumping in the car for school or work. To make this breakfast gluten-free, use your favorite gluten-free bread instead of the pita pockets. You can also make these pockets with baked ham or leave the meat out altogether and add chopped spinach or tomatoes instead.

Cooking spray
4 large eggs, lightly beaten
2 teaspoons honey mustard
¼ teaspoon freshly ground black pepper
4 ounces smoked turkey, diced
4 ounces Swiss cheese, shredded or diced
2 whole wheat pita pockets, halved crosswise

Coat a large skillet with cooking spray and preheat over medium-high heat.

Whisk together the eggs, honey mustard, and pepper. Add the mixture to the hot pan. Stir in the turkey and cheese and cook until the eggs are cooked through and the cheese melts, stirring frequently. Spoon the egg mixture into the pita pockets.

Egg Salad with Roasted Red Peppers on Toasted Mini Bagels

Serves 4 ■ Prep time: 15 to 20 minutes

I love the smoky sweetness that roasted red peppers add to egg salad. You could also add pimentos or oil-packed sun-dried tomatoes for the same effect. The egg salad also makes a great school lunch—just keep it chilled with an ice pack. The egg salad can be made up to 2 days in advance and refrigerated until ready to serve.

Nutrients per serving:
Calories: 201
Fat: 10g
Saturated Fat: 2g
Cholesterol: 185mg
Carbohydrate: 17g
Protein: 9g
Fiber: 1g
Sodium: 380mg

4 large eggs
¼ cup light mayonnaise
¼ cup diced roasted red peppers
¼ teaspoon dry mustard
Salt and freshly ground black pepper
4 mini bagels, sliced and lightly toasted

Place the eggs in a large saucepan and pour over enough cold water to cover the eggs by about 2 inches. Set the pan over high heat and bring to a boil. Boil for 12 minutes. Drain and immediately plunge the eggs into ice-cold water.

When cool enough to handle, remove the shells from the eggs and chop the eggs into small pieces. Transfer the eggs to a large bowl and stir in the mayonnaise, red peppers, and dry mustard. Mix well. Season to taste with salt and pepper.

Spoon the egg salad onto the bagels and serve open-faced or as sandwiches.

One-Egg Western Omelet

Serves 1 ■ Prep time: 10 minutes

The salsa in this omelet is the perfect addition to the traditional Western (or Denver) omelet: eggs with onions and bell peppers. Pick your favorite brand and enjoy a restaurant-style breakfast in minutes. Instead of ham, you can add 2 slices cooked and crumbled center-cut bacon. For a meat-free version, simply eliminate the ham and add sliced mushrooms instead.

Nutrients per serving:
Calories: 195
Fat: 10.5g
Saturated Fat: 5g
Cholesterol: 209mg
Carbohydrate: 6g
Protein: 17g
Fiber: <1g
Sodium: 585mg

Cooking spray
1 large egg
2 tablespoons low-fat (1%) milk
2 tablespoons salsa of your choice
2 tablespoons shredded Mexican cheese blend or sharp cheddar cheese
1 slice (about 1 ounce) smoked ham, chopped

Coat a small skillet with cooking spray and preheat over medium-high heat.

Whisk together the egg, milk, and salsa and add to the hot pan. Cook for 1 to 2 minutes, until the bottom of the egg mixture is cooked, lifting up the sides and allowing any uncooked egg mixture to slide to the bottom of the pan. Using a spatula, flip the egg mixture (as if flipping a pancake).

Top one half of the omelet with the cheese and ham. Fold the untopped side over the cheese and ham and cook for 30 seconds to 1 minute, until the cheese melts.

Curried Potato "Chips" with Over-Medium Eggs

Serves 2 ■ Prep time: 10 to 15 minutes ■ Cooking time: 20 to 25 minutes

These are, by far, my son Kyle's favorite potato "chips." He always asks for a batch "with curry" when I'm making potatoes. I love the combination of smoky curry with a freshly cooked egg. Kyle likes them with ketchup, too. If you want to slice the potatoes in advance, soak them in cold water (for up to 24 hours) to prevent browning. The chips can also be baked up to 24 hours in advance and stored in the refrigerator. Reheat the chips in a single layer on a baking sheet for 10 minutes at 300°F. To serve more than one, simply double, triple, or quadruple the recipe.

Nutrients per serving:
Calories: 168
Fat: 4g
Saturated Fat: 1g
Cholesterol: 180mg
Carbohydrate: 22g
Protein: 9g
Fiber: 1g
Sodium: 77mg

Cooking spray
1 large or 2 small Yukon gold potatoes, sliced ⅛ inch thick
¼ teaspoon curry powder
Salt and freshly ground black pepper
2 large eggs

Preheat the oven to 375°F. Coat a large baking sheet with cooking spray.

Arrange the potato slices on the prepared baking sheet. Spray the potato slices with cooking spray and sprinkle the curry powder over the top. Season the potatoes to taste with salt and pepper. Bake for 20 to 25 minutes, until golden brown.

Coat a large skillet with cooking spray and preheat over medium-high. Add the eggs and cook for 1 to 2 minutes, until the whites are cooked through. Using a spatula, flip the eggs (being careful not to break the yolks) and cook for 30 more seconds, or until the yolks are almost cooked through (or longer for fully cooked eggs). Arrange the chips on plates and top with the cooked eggs.

Breakfast Pizza with Ricotta & Canadian Bacon

Serves 1 ■ Prep time: 10 minutes ■ Cooking time: 10 minutes

Nutrients per serving:
Calories: 202
Fat: 8g
Saturated Fat: 3g
Cholesterol: 27mg
Carbohydrate: 19g
Protein: 13g
Fiber: 1g
Sodium: 693mg

Imagine a revamped Hawaiian pizza for breakfast. This creative breakfast boasts a tortilla crust topped with oregano-spiked ricotta cheese, salty Canadian bacon, and nutty Parmesan cheese. It's the ultimate sweet and savory flavor combination. For added sweetness and true Hawaiian inspiration, add ¼ cup diced fresh or canned pineapple (canned in 100 percent juice). The breakfast pizza can be assembled and refrigerated up to 24 hours in advance and baked just before serving. For a gluten-free meal, opt for a gluten-free tortilla.

Cooking spray

1 fajita-size flour tortilla (regular or whole wheat)

2 tablespoons part-skim ricotta cheese

¼ teaspoon dried oregano

⅛ teaspoon freshly ground black pepper

¼ cup diced Canadian bacon

2 teaspoons grated Parmesan cheese

Preheat the oven to 375°F. Coat a baking sheet with cooking spray.

Place the tortilla on a flat surface. Whisk together the ricotta, oregano, and black pepper. Spread the mixture all over the tortilla, to within ½ inch of the edges. Top the ricotta with the Canadian bacon and Parmesan. Bake for 10 minutes, or until the top is golden brown.

Buttermilk Flapjacks with Bacon

Serves 8 ■ Prep time: 10 minutes ■ Cooking time: 5 to 10 minutes

Bacon shouldn't always be relegated to the side of the plate. My son Luke adores the smoky meat, and I created these tender buttermilk flapjacks so he could enjoy a hint of bacon in every delicious mouthful (he enjoys a three-stack with a drizzle of warm maple syrup). My boys also love cheddar cheese, so for cheesy flapjacks, add ½ cup shredded sharp cheddar cheese to the batter. The flapjack batter can be made up to 24 hours in advance and refrigerated until ready to cook. Don't worry that this recipe serves 8, because you can either store leftover batter in the refrigerator and cook more flapjacks the following morning, or you can cook all the flapjacks at once and reheat the leftovers in the microwave (for about 15 seconds). When making large batches of flapjacks, keep the finished flapjacks warm in a 200°F oven until ready to serve.

Nutrients per serving:
Calories: 154
Fat: 2g
Saturated Fat: 1g
Cholesterol: 29mg
Carbohydrate: 27g
Protein: 6g
Fiber: 1g
Sodium: 315mg

Cooking spray
2 cups all-purpose flour
3 teaspoons baking powder
¼ teaspoon salt
1¼ cups low-fat buttermilk
1 large egg
4 slices center-cut bacon, cooked until crisp and crumbled

Coat a large griddle or skillet with cooking spray and preheat over medium-high heat.

In a large bowl, whisk together the flour, baking powder, and salt. Make a well in the center. Whisk together the buttermilk and egg and add to the well in the flour mixture. Mix gently to combine, leaving any small lumps. Fold in the bacon.

Ladle the batter onto the hot griddle (about ¼ cup per flapjack) and cook for 1 to 2 minutes, until tiny bubbles appear around the edges of the flapjacks. Flip the flapjacks and cook for 15 to 30 more seconds, until cooked through.

Mini Blueberry Pancakes

Serves 8 ■ Prep time: 10 minutes ■ Cooking time: 5 to 10 minutes

There are few foods more comforting than warm pancakes bursting with fresh fruit. And pancakes are super kid friendly because you can create shapes with the batter and faces with the fruit, like blueberry eyes, a banana nose, and a strawberry mouth. Have fun and get the kids to help. This recipe is super versatile, so feel free to substitute another fruit for the blueberries (raspberries or sliced bananas are terrific).

The pancake batter can be made up to 24 hours in advance and refrigerated until ready to cook. This makes a big batch, so you can either store leftover batter in the refrigerator and cook more pancakes the following morning, or you can cook all the pancakes at once and reheat the leftovers in the microwave (for about 15 seconds).

Nutrients per serving:
Calories: 152
Fat: 1g
Saturated Fat: <1g
Cholesterol: 25mg
Carbohydrate: 29g
Protein: 6g
Fiber: 1g
Sodium: 248mg

Cooking spray
2 cups all-purpose flour
3 teaspoons baking powder
¼ teaspoon salt
1¼ cups low-fat (1%) milk
1 large egg
1 cup unsweetened frozen blueberries

Coat a large griddle or skillet with cooking spray and preheat over medium-high heat.

In a large bowl, whisk together the flour, baking powder, and salt. Make a well in the center. Whisk together the milk and egg and add to the well in the flour mixture. Mix gently to combine, leaving any small lumps. Fold in the frozen blueberries.

Ladle the batter onto the hot pan (about 2 tablespoons per pancake) and cook for 1 to 2 minutes, until tiny bubbles appear around the edges of the pancakes. Flip the pancakes and cook for 15 to 30 more seconds, until cooked through.

Apple Cinnamon Pancakes

Serves 4 ■ Prep time: 10 minutes ■ Cooking time: 5 minutes

Apples and cinnamon have a natural affinity, and when you add both to pancake batter, the result is a warm and wonderful way to start the day. These flapjacks are fluffy and loaded with flavor thanks to fresh apple cider and ground cinnamon. Start with your favorite pancake mix, and then jazz things up with just a few extra ingredients. The pancake batter can be made up to 24 hours in advance and refrigerated until ready to serve (that means you can wake up in the morning, flip pancakes, and head out the door well fed and energized). For the maple syrup, I like to warm mine in the microwave for about 20 seconds on HIGH power before drizzling it over a short stack! When making large batches of pancakes, keep the finished pancakes warm in a 200°F oven until ready to serve.

Nutrients per serving:

Calories: 346

Fat: 3g

Saturated Fat: <1g

Cholesterol: 14mg

Carbohydrate: 72g

Protein: 7g

Fiber: 2g

Sodium: 801mg

Cooking spray

2 cups pancake mix of your choice

1½ cups fresh apple cider

1 teaspoon ground cinnamon

1 teaspoon vanilla extract

4 tablespoons pure maple syrup, or more as desired

Coat a griddle with cooking spray and preheat over medium-high heat.

In a large bowl, whisk together the pancake mix, apple cider, cinnamon, and vanilla until blended, leaving any small lumps.

Ladle the batter onto the hot griddle (about ¼ cup per pancake) and cook for 1 to 2 minutes, until tiny bubbles appear around the edges of the pancakes. Flip the pancakes and cook for 15 to 30 more seconds, until cooked through. Serve the pancakes with the maple syrup drizzled over the top.

Pumpernickel Squares with Vegetable Cream Cheese

Serves 4 ■ Prep time: 10 minutes

Nutrients per serving:
Calories: 127
Fat: 6g
Saturated Fat: 2.6g
Cholesterol: 13mg
Carbohydrate: 16g
Protein: 4g
Fiber: 2g
Sodium: 500mg

Pumpernickel squares are overlooked at breakfast time. That's a shame, because the dark bread has a unique, tangy flavor that partners exceptionally well with both sweet and savory foods. In this recipe, I top thin slices of pumpernickel with vegetable cream cheese, salty olives, and fresh spinach. It's a savory breakfast that also makes a great afternoon snack. For a fun, kid-friendly presentation, create a face or polka dot pattern with the olive slices. For finicky eaters, spread the cream cheese mixture on whole grain crackers, "pretzel" crackers, or bagel chips. For adults who want added flair, add thinly sliced smoked salmon on top just before serving.

The cream cheese mixture can be made up to 24 hours in advance and refrigerated until ready to spread on the bread.

4 ounces light vegetable cream cheese, softened
½ cup chopped baby spinach
4 slices pumpernickel bread, cut into 4 squares each
¼ cup pimento-stuffed green olives, thinly sliced

Whisk together the cream cheese and spinach until blended. Spread the cream cheese mixture onto the pumpernickel squares. Top with the sliced olives.

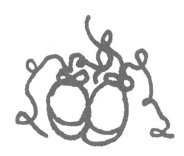

Cinnamon Rolls with Brown Sugar & Walnuts

Serves 12 ■ Prep time: 10 to 15 minutes ■ Cooking time: 20 to 25 minutes

Sleepovers at the Miller house wouldn't be complete without my signature cinnamon rolls for breakfast. Adults and kids alike are speechless when their lips meet the warm, cinnamon- and brown sugar–spiked rolls drizzled with sweet glaze. And speechless is good after a night of little boys running around the house! I especially like this recipe for hectic mornings because I can prep the rolls the night before (or up to 24 hours ahead) and refrigerate them overnight.

If desired, you can make the cinnamon rolls without any nuts or replace the walnuts with pecans. For a citrus-flavored glaze, substitute 2 teaspoons orange juice for the water. Since there's virtually no fat in this recipe, the cinnamon rolls don't stay moist for days on end. It's a good thing they're addicting, because you should try to eat them within 24 to 48 hours (never a problem in my house). For larger groups, simply double or triple the recipe and fill more cake pans.

Nutrients per serving:
Calories: 147
Fat: 4g
Saturated Fat: 0g
Cholesterol: 0mg
Carbohydrate: 25g
Protein: 4g
Fiber: 1g
Sodium: 213mg

Cooking spray
1 pound frozen bread dough, thawed according to package directions
¼ cup packed light brown sugar
½ teaspoon ground cinnamon
⅓ cup finely chopped walnuts
¼ cup confectioners' sugar

Preheat the oven to 350°F. Coat two 9-inch round cake pans with cooking spray.

Roll the bread dough out into a rectangle about ⅛ inch thick and about 12 by 15 inches in diameter. Spread the brown sugar all over the dough, to within ⅛ inch of the edges. Sprinkle the cinnamon over the brown sugar and top with the walnuts.

Starting with the shorter end, roll up the dough tightly. Using a sharp knife, cut the roll crosswise into twelve 1-inch-thick rounds. Place the rounds into the bottom of the prepared cake pans (6 per pan), leaving space between the rolls to allow room for expansion. Bake for 20 to 25 minutes, until the rolls are puffed up and golden brown.

Meanwhile, whisk together the confectioners' sugar and 2 teaspoons water. Drizzle the glaze over the baked cinnamon rolls and serve warm or at room temperature.

Almond Coffee Cake

Serves 8 ■ Prep time: 10 minutes ■ Cooking time: 35 to 40 minutes
Cooling time: 10 minutes

Nutrients per serving:
Calories: 381
Fat: 4.5g
Saturated Fat: 2g
Cholesterol: 64mg
Carbohydrate: 72g
Protein: 13g
Fiber: 3g
Sodium: 558mg

This moist cake is extra sweet and nutty thanks to sweetened condensed milk and almond extract. It's also a healthy choice because I use fat-free condensed milk and light sour cream. Consider it a decadent pound cake without the extra pounds. I think it's a great addition to a brunch birthday party because both adults and kids will find it tantalizing. Plus, you can bake the cake up to 24 hours in advance and store it at room temperature or in the refrigerator until party time. For a fancy presentation, top the coffee cake with confectioners' sugar, toasted slivered almonds, and fresh raspberries. For variety, use vanilla or orange extract instead of almond extract. For larger groups, simply double or triple the recipe and make two to three cakes.

Cooking spray
2 cups biscuit mix
1 (14-ounce) can fat-free sweetened condensed milk
1 cup light sour cream
2 large eggs
1 teaspoon almond extract

Preheat the oven to 350°F. Coat an 11 by 7-inch baking dish with cooking spray.

In a large bowl, whisk together the biscuit mix, sweetened condensed milk, sour cream, eggs, and almond extract.

Pour the mixture into the prepared pan and bake for 35 to 40 minutes, until a wooden pick inserted near the center comes out clean.

Cool the cake in the pan on a wire rack for 10 minutes before cutting into squares.

Overnight Vanilla Bread Pudding

Serves 6 ■ Prep time: 10 minutes ■ Cooking time: 45 minutes

Call me crazy, but I downright worship bread pudding. I love turning my favorite French or Italian day-old (or several-day-old) bread into a spectacular, warm breakfast for family and friends. When the bread is slightly stale and dry, it absorbs all the flavors of the ingredients you partner it with and it comes back to life in a moist and magical way. I especially like this bread pudding recipe because you can do all the prep work the night before and bake the dish in the morning. It can be a hectic school morning or a lazy Sunday brunch—it's welcome any time. For added flavor, add 1 teaspoon of ground cinnamon to the milk mixture. For added color and texture, sprinkle ½ cup of dried cherries over the bread pieces before pouring over the milk mixture.

8 ounces French bread (or ½ loaf), cut or broken up into 1-inch pieces

1½ cups low-fat (1%) milk

1 (14-ounce) can fat-free sweetened condensed milk

4 large eggs

1 teaspoon vanilla extract

Arrange the bread cubes in a shallow baking dish (11 by 7-inch or 13 by 9-inch).

In a large bowl, whisk together the milk, condensed milk, eggs, and vanilla. Pour the mixture all over the bread. Press down to cover the bread with the milk mixture. Cover the dish with plastic, pressing down slightly to cover the bread with the milk mixture. Refrigerate up to 24 hours.

Preheat the oven to 350°F.

Remove the plastic from the baking dish and bake the bread pudding for 45 minutes, until the top is golden brown and the milk mixture is set.

CHILLED
Chicken Caesar Pita Pocket
Soba Noodles with Edamame & Soy
Hawaiian Chicken Salad with Pineapple & Pepper Jack
Turkey Wraps with Avocado & Sun-Dried Tomato Spread
Rice Salad with Smoked Turkey & Raisins
Honey Ham & Romaine on Ciabatta
Tuna Salad on Whole Grain Crackers
School-Time Cobb
Italian Antipasti
Olive-Spiked Hummus with Pita

WARM
Chicken Tortilla Soup
Chunky Tomato Soup & Cheese Sandwich Roll-Ups
Creamy Corn Chowder
Cheese "Fondue" with Whole Grain Bread Cubes
White Cheddar Mac 'n' Cheese

ROOM TEMPERATURE (ICE PACK OPTIONAL)
Penne with Tomatoes, Basil & Cubed Mozzarella
Zucchini-Havarti Panini with Fig Jam
Strawberry-Cucumber Salad with Hazelnuts
Ham & Swiss Wraps with Apricot Preserves
Nut Butter & Fruit Preserve Cracker Sandwiches
Corn, Tomato & Avocado Salad
Hummus & Bell Pepper "Sushi" on Lavash
Grilled Portobello & Pesto Pita Pockets
Mushroom & Spinach Quesadillas
Lemony Sweet Pea Risotto
Quinoa Salad with Black Beans, Corn & Cilantro
French Bread Pizza with Mozzarella & Parmesan

CHAPTER 2

Lunch for School and Work

Chicken Caesar Pita Pocket

Serves 1 ■ Prep time: 10 minutes

Garlic- and Parmesan-spiked Caesar dressing is an excellent partner for mild-flavored chicken. I promise this is not your average chicken salad. In fact, I add extra Parmesan cheese so you can truly taste it. When it comes to the dressing, select your favorite brand and try to stick to a reduced-calorie, lower-fat variety. For the salad, feel free to add additional ingredients, such as diced celery, red onion, and sun-dried tomatoes. If you've got lots of mouths to feed, this recipe is easy to double, triple, and quadruple so that the whole family can enjoy a great meal, whether at school, at work, or at home.

Perfect for make-ahead lunches, the chicken salad can be made up to 24 hours in advance and refrigerated until ready to stuff into the pita pocket.

Nutrients per serving:
Calories: 379
Fat: 12g
Saturated Fat: 3g
Cholesterol: 126mg
Carbohydrate: 20g
Protein: 47g
Fiber: 2g
Sodium: 559mg

- **1 cup cubed cooked chicken breast (poached, grilled, roasted, or rotisserie)**
- **1 tablespoon light mayonnaise**
- **1 tablespoon light Caesar dressing**
- **1 teaspoon grated Parmesan cheese**
- **Salt and freshly ground black pepper**
- **1 whole wheat pita pocket, halved crosswise**

In a medium bowl, combine the chicken, mayonnaise, Caesar dressing, and Parmesan. Mix well and season to taste with salt and pepper.

Spoon the chicken salad into the pita pocket and serve, or wrap in plastic wrap and refrigerate until ready to serve.

Soba Noodles with Edamame & Soy

Serves 4 ■ Prep time: 10 to 15 minutes

Soba noodles are hearty buckwheat noodles with a subtle nutty flavor that stands up to a variety of bold flavors and textures. In this dish, I partner the softened noodles with crisp-tender edamame, soy sauce, and sesame oil. Fresh cilantro adds a burst of freshness and color. I love this dish because you can serve it warm, at room temperature, or chilled. That means that it's ready any time. If you want to make the dish tonight and already have whole wheat spaghetti on hand, you can substitute that for the soba noodles. If you want to plan ahead for future meals, you can make this dish up to 24 hours in advance and refrigerate it until ready to serve.

Nutrients per serving:
Calories: 248
Fat: 4g
Saturated Fat: <1g
Cholesterol: 0mg
Carbohydrate: 45g
Protein: 12g
Fiber: 1g
Sodium: 646mg

8 ounces soba noodles

1 cup shelled edamame (soybeans)

2 tablespoons chopped fresh cilantro

2 tablespoons reduced-sodium soy sauce

2 teaspoons toasted sesame oil

Cook the noodles according to the package directions. Drain and transfer the noodles to a large bowl. Add the remaining ingredients and mix well. Refrigerate the noodles until ready to serve or pack for lunch.

Hawaiian Chicken Salad with Pineapple & Pepper Jack

Serves 1 ■ Prep time: 10 to 15 minutes

Kids love the sweetness of pineapple paired with the chicken in this salad. Most folks also like the pairing of sweet pineapple with mildly hot pepper Jack cheese but, for finicky eaters, you can use regular Monterey Jack cheese instead of pepper Jack. Cheddar cheese works well, too. I add parsley because it lends great color and brings out the flavor of all the other ingredients. The chicken salad can be made up to 24 hours in advance and refrigerated until ready to serve or pack for lunch.

Nutrients per serving:
Calories: 463
Fat: 24g
Saturated Fat: 8g
Cholesterol: 160mg
Carbohydrate: 9g
Protein: 50g
Fiber: 1g
Sodium: 517mg

1 cup cubed cooked chicken breast (poached, grilled, roasted, or rotisserie)

¼ cup diced pineapple (fresh or canned in 100% juice)

¼ cup diced pepper Jack cheese

2 tablespoons light mayonnaise

1 tablespoon chopped fresh parsley

Salt and freshly ground black pepper

In a medium bowl, combine the chicken, pineapple, cheese, mayonnaise, and parsley. Mix well and season to taste with salt and pepper. Refrigerate the chicken salad until ready to serve.

Turkey Wraps with Avocado & Sun-Dried Tomato Spread

Serves 2 ■ Prep time: 10 to 15 minutes

This tomato-spiked avocado spread is an excellent partner for smoked turkey and Swiss cheese. In fact, it's also great on crackers, as a topping for baked or roasted fish, or as a dip for steamed or grilled shrimp. When I make these wraps, I often add baby spinach or red leaf lettuce for added nutrients, flavor, and color. If you want to swap ingredients, you may also make this wrap with smoked or baked ham or deli-style sliced chicken breast. For a meat-free version, simply add more Swiss cheese or use a combination of cheeses. If the sodium count is too high for your liking, select reduced-sodium turkey and cheese varieties.

Nutrients per serving:
Calories: 435
Fat: 27g
Saturated Fat: 9g
Cholesterol: 57mg
Carbohydrate: 32g
Protein: 23g
Fiber: 8g
Sodium: 799mg

1 ripe avocado, pitted, peeled, and diced

2 teaspoons sun-dried tomato paste

2 fajita-size flour tortillas (regular or whole wheat)

4 ounces smoked or roasted turkey breast, thinly sliced

2 slices Swiss cheese

In a medium bowl, combine the avocado and sun-dried tomato paste. Using a fork, mix the two ingredients together until the tomato paste is completely blended with the avocado.

Spread the avocado mixture on one side of the tortillas, to within ¼ inch of the edges. Top the avocado mixture with the turkey slices and Swiss cheese. Roll up tightly, wrap with plastic wrap, and refrigerate until ready to serve.

Rice Salad with Smoked Turkey & Raisins

Serves 4 ■ Prep time: 20 minutes

I got creative with rice one day and ended up with this great invention! Smoked turkey, sweet raisins, and tangy vinegar are at home in a hearty, rice-based salad. You should get creative, too, especially when making the meal for finicky folks. Try adding grapes, cubed cheese, or diced cucumber. To save time, use the microwavable brown rice sold in pouches. White rice works too (use leftover rice from Chinese takeout to save time).

The rice salad can be made up to 24 hours in advance and refrigerated until ready to serve or pack for lunch.

Nutrients per serving:
Calories: 245
Fat: 5g
Saturated Fat: 1g
Cholesterol: 4mg
Carbohydrate: 45g
Protein: 6g
Fiber: 2g
Sodium: 85mg

1 cup brown rice
1 cup diced smoked turkey
¼ cup raisins
¼ cup chopped fresh parsley
2 tablespoons sherry vinegar
1 tablespoon olive oil
Salt and freshly ground black pepper

Cook the rice according to the package directions.

Stir in the turkey, raisins, parsley, vinegar, and oil. Season to taste with salt and pepper. Refrigerate until ready to serve.

Honey Ham & Romaine on Ciabatta

Serves 1 ■ Prep time: 10 minutes

I love the combination of salty ham and creamy Babybel cheese, especially on chewy ciabatta bread. The addition of honey mustard and crunchy lettuce makes this a sandwich you'll be packing over and over again. For variety, you could also use a mild cheddar or fontina cheese. If you've got finicky eaters, turkey or chicken would be great alternatives to the ham. Or, some kids might want to go "meat-free." If that's the case, add another round of Babybel (that's the way my son Luke likes it).

1 individual ciabatta roll
2 teaspoons honey mustard
1 ounce baked honey ham or smoked ham
1 Babybel cheese round, thinly sliced
1 leaf romaine lettuce

Nutrients per serving:
Calories: 262
Fat: 12g
Saturated Fat: 6g
Cholesterol: 39mg
Carbohydrate: 25g
Protein: 17g
Fiber: 1g
Sodium: 619mg

Halve the ciabatta roll horizontally (through the equator). Spread the honey mustard on the inside of the roll and top the bottom half with the ham, cheese, and lettuce. Wrap in plastic wrap and refrigerate until ready to serve.

Lunch Box Additions

The following items make excellent additions to the lunch box for school and work. They can be eaten with the main meal or saved for "snack time."

Baby carrots

Celery sticks

Zucchini sticks

Cantaloupe, honeydew, and watermelon (cubed or scooped with a melon baller)

Dried and dehydrated fruits and vegetables: raisins, cranberries, cherries, mango, pineapple, apricots, blueberries, bananas, papaya, tomatoes, peas, corn

Nuts: almonds, cashews, peanuts, pistachios, pecans, walnuts

Pretzel sticks with peanut butter

Fruit-filled cookies (such as Fig Newtons)

Granola bars

Rice cakes with cottage cheese

Baked corn chips with salsa and/or bean dip

Pickles

Olives

Fruit leather

Unsweetened applesauce

Pudding

Yogurt

Graham cracker sandwiches with hazelnut spread

Whole grain, low-sugar cereal

Tuna Salad on Whole Grain Crackers

Serves 1 ■ Prep time: 10 to 15 minutes

Tuna salad is truly a matter of personal experience and preference. We like ours with crisp celery, smoky roasted red peppers, and lots of black pepper. Sometimes I even add diced pickles or Greek olives. Feel free to add or delete ingredients to suit your family's desires.

The tuna salad can be made up to 24 hours in advance and refrigerated until ready to serve or pack for lunch.

Nutrients per serving:
Calories: 346
Fat: 14g
Saturated Fat: 3g
Cholesterol: 26mg
Carbohydrate: 35g
Protein: 22g
Fiber: 5g
Sodium: 671mg

1 (2.6-ounce) packet light tuna in water
1 tablespoon light mayonnaise
1 tablespoon finely diced celery
1 tablespoon finely diced roasted red peppers
Salt and freshly ground black pepper
6 whole grain crackers (such as Triscuits)

In a small bowl, combine the tuna and mayonnaise and mix well. Fold in the celery and red peppers. Season to taste with salt and pepper.

Serve the tuna salad on the crackers, or refrigerate the tuna salad until ready to serve.

School-Time Cobb

Serves 4 ■ Prep time: 10 to 15 minutes

For this salad, I love to mix and match ingredients. This version has crisp cucumber, sharp cheese, and Greek olives, but I often add chopped ham or turkey, chunks of tuna, crumbled bacon, and diced hard-boiled eggs. You can also add a variety of fresh vegetables, such as carrots, tomatoes, broccoli florets, and bell peppers. When packing it for lunch, pack the dressing on the side so the lettuce stays crisp. If you don't want to deal with two separate containers (one for the salad and one for the dressing), spoon the dressing into the bottom of the container before topping with the lettuce and remaining ingredients. When you're ready to eat, simply toss the salad from the bottom of the container, mixing until all the ingredients are coated.

Nutrients per serving:
Calories: 281
Fat: 25g
Saturated Fat: 9g
Cholesterol: 50mg
Carbohydrate: 3g
Protein: 9g
Fiber: 1g
Sodium: 642mg

4 cups chopped romaine lettuce

1 cup diced English (seedless) cucumber

1 cup diced sharp cheddar cheese (or other favorite cheese, such as Swiss, crumbled blue, or feta)

¼ cup sliced black olives (preferably Greek)

1 cup light ranch dressing

Arrange the lettuce in the bottom of a sealable plastic container. Top with the cucumber, cheese, and olives. Spoon the dressing into a separate container. Refrigerate the salad and dressing until ready to serve.

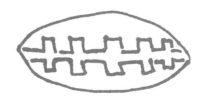

Italian Antipasti

Serves 4 ■ Prep time: 10 minutes

This colorful feast is brimming with bold flavor thanks to the turkey pepperoni and olives. I partnered those ingredients with sweet red bell pepper and mild mozzarella cheese. Feel free to add additional ingredients, such as shaved Parmesan cheese, pickled banana peppers, and thinly sliced prosciutto. And when I don't have a fresh bell pepper handy, I often substitute roasted red peppers. If you can find lunch containers with individual compartments, they work best for this fabulous meal.

To reduce the amount of sodium in this recipe, opt for reduced-sodium or unsalted crackers.

Nutrients per serving:
Calories: 244
Fat: 11g
Saturated Fat: 5g
Cholesterol: 50mg
Carbohydrate: 18g
Protein: 19g
Fiber: 2g
Sodium: 758mg

- **1 cup sliced turkey pepperoni**
- **4 ounces part-skim mozzarella cheese, thinly sliced**
- **1 cup pitted olives (any variety)**
- **1 red bell pepper, seeded and thinly sliced**
- **24 melba toast crackers**

Assemble the pepperoni, cheese, olives, and red bell pepper in a sealable plastic container and refrigerate until ready to serve. Pack the crackers in a separate container or plastic bag.

Olive-Spiked Hummus with Pita

Serves 4 ■ Prep time: 10 to 15 minutes

Nutrients per serving:
Calories: 291
Fat: 9g
Saturated Fat: 1g
Cholesterol: 0mg
Carbohydrate: 45g
Protein: 11g
Fiber: 9g
Sodium: 691mg

This hummus is great for parties and is popular with adults and kids. It's simple to prepare because you just jazz up prepared hummus with olives, capers, and bright green parsley. It's like blending hummus with olive tapenade. For a change from the pita, serve the hummus with bagel chips, pretzels, baby carrots, zucchini sticks, celery, and/or bell pepper strips.

The hummus can be made up to 24 hours in advance and refrigerated until ready to serve or pack for lunch. For larger groups, simply double or triple the recipe. For a gluten-free meal, serve the hummus with fresh vegetables or gluten-free crackers.

1 cup plain hummus

6 Greek olives, pitted

2 teaspoons drained capers

2 tablespoons chopped fresh parsley

4 whole wheat pita pockets, cut into 6 wedges each

In a blender, combine the hummus, olives, and capers. Puree until smooth and blended. Fold in the parsley. Refrigerate until ready to serve or pack for lunch.

Serve the hummus with the pita wedges on the side for dipping.

Chicken Tortilla Soup

Serves 4 ■ Prep time: 5 minutes ■ Cooking time: 10 minutes

This soup is crammed with flavor and texture. I love to use the salsa from my favorite Mexican restaurant, so whenever we dine there, I order extra salsa to go. Use your favorite salsa in your version. For the cooked chicken, use a deli rotisserie chicken, or cut up leftover roasted or grilled chicken.

The soup can be made up to 24 hours in advance and refrigerated until ready to reheat and serve or pack in a Thermos for lunch. To keep the corn chips crisp, add them to the soup just before eating.

Nutrients per serving:
Calories: 231
Fat: 4g
Saturated Fat: 1g
Cholesterol: 60mg
Carbohydrate: 22g
Protein: 25g
Fiber: 5g
Sodium: 667mg

1 (28-ounce) can diced tomatoes, undrained

2 cups shredded or cubed cooked chicken breast (poached, grilled, roasted, or rotisserie)

1 cup prepared salsa of your choice

¼ cup chopped fresh cilantro

1 cup crumbled baked corn tortilla chips

In a medium saucepan, combine the tomatoes, chicken, and salsa. Set the pan over medium heat and bring to a simmer. Decrease the heat to low and simmer for 10 minutes. Remove the pan from the heat and stir in the cilantro.

Ladle the soup into bowls and top with the tortilla chips.

Chunky Tomato Soup & Cheese Sandwich Roll-Ups

Serves 4 ■ Prep time: 5 to 10 minutes ■ Cooking time: 10 minutes

This fun soup blends chunks of canned tomatoes with creamy evaporated milk. Fresh basil makes everything taste clean and bright. For the roll-ups, use your favorite cheese variety. In my family, Kyle likes pepper Jack, Luke likes American, and I like Swiss.

The soup can be made up to 24 hours in advance and refrigerated until ready to reheat and either serve or pack in a Thermos for lunch.

2 (14-ounce) cans petite diced tomatoes, undrained
1 (12-ounce) can evaporated skim milk
2 tablespoons chopped fresh basil
Salt and freshly ground black pepper
4 slices whole wheat bread
4 slices American cheese

Nutrients per serving:
Calories: 217
Fat: 4g
Saturated Fat: 2g
Cholesterol: 11mg
Carbohydrate: 33g
Protein: 13g
Fiber: 5g
Sodium: 673mg

In a medium saucepan, combine the tomatoes and milk. Set the pan over medium-high heat and bring to a simmer. Decrease the heat to medium and simmer for 10 minutes. Remove the pan from the heat and stir in the basil. Season to taste with salt and pepper.

Arrange the bread slices on a flat surface. Using a rolling pin, roll the bread slices out until $1/8$ inch thick. Top each bread slice with a slice of cheese. Roll up tightly, wrap in plastic wrap, and refrigerate the roll-ups until ready to serve or pack for lunch.

Creamy Corn Chowder

Serves 4 ■ Prep time: 5 to 10 minutes ■ Cooking time: 10 minutes

I adore creamed corn. It's sweet and rich and the perfect base for soup. To develop a deeper flavor for this chowder, I added red bell pepper, bay leaves, and onion. For a more decadent version, top each serving with 3 tablespoons fresh lump crabmeat. Crazy good.

The chowder can be made up to 24 hours in advance and refrigerated until ready to reheat and serve or pack in a Thermos for lunch.

2 (14.75-ounce) cans creamed corn
2 (12-ounce) cans evaporated skim milk
1 red bell pepper, seeded and chopped
2 bay leaves
1 teaspoon dried minced onion
Salt and freshly ground black pepper

In a medium saucepan, combine the creamed corn, milk, bell pepper, bay leaves, and dried onion. Set the pan over medium-high heat and bring to a simmer. Decrease the heat to medium and simmer for 10 minutes. Season to taste with salt and pepper. Remove the bay leaves before serving.

Cheese "Fondue" with Whole Grain Bread Cubes

Serves 4 ■ Prep time: 20 minutes

Nutrients per serving:
Calories: 430
Fat: 18g
Saturated Fat: 10g
Cholesterol: 56mg
Carbohydrate: 41g
Protein: 28g
Fiber: 4g
Sodium: 492mg

My mom made fondue all the time when I was growing up. The smell of gooey, melted cheese spiked with Dijon mustard brings me back to my childhood in a flash. And fondues are super versatile because you can serve practically anything on the side for dunking. For birthday parties (for kids or adults), serve the fondue with baby carrots, celery sticks, zucchini slices, and bell pepper strips in addition to the bread cubes. For larger groups, simply double or triple the recipe.

The fondue and bread cubes can be made up to 24 hours in advance. Refrigerate the fondue until ready to reheat and serve. The bread cubes can be kept at room temperature.

8 slices whole grain bread

8 ounces Swiss or Gruyère cheese, shredded, or a combination of the two

1 tablespoon cornstarch or all-purpose flour

1 (12-ounce) can evaporated skim milk

½ teaspoon Dijon mustard

Salt and freshly ground black pepper

Toast the bread slices and cut into bite-size squares or thin strips. Set aside.

Combine the cheese and cornstarch in a large freezer bag and shake to coat the cheese with the cornstarch.

Heat the milk and mustard together in a medium saucepan over medium heat. When tiny bubbles appear around the edges of the pan, gradually stir in the cheese. Simmer until the cheese melts and the mixture is smooth, stirring constantly. Remove from the heat and season to taste with salt and pepper.

Serve, or refrigerate the fondue until ready to reheat and serve.

White Cheddar Mac 'n' Cheese

Serves 4 ■ Prep time: 20 to 25 minutes

This mac 'n' cheese is both creamy and bold. The sharp cheddar cheese adds the ideal amount of nuttiness to the dish, and the evaporated milk makes the sauce much richer than it would be with regular skim milk. I often spruce up my mac 'n' cheese with diced sun-dried tomatoes, roasted red peppers, or pimento because they add color and sweetness. If your mixture becomes stiff after being refrigerated, add a little skim milk, evaporated skim milk, or water when reheating to loosen it.

The mac 'n' cheese can be made up to 24 hours in advance and refrigerated until ready to reheat and serve or pack in an insulated container for lunch.

Nutrients per serving:
Calories: 617
Fat: 23g
Saturated Fat: 13g
Cholesterol: 64mg
Carbohydrate: 72g
Protein: 30g
Fiber: 3g
Sodium: 467mg

> **12 ounces elbow macaroni**
> **1 (12-ounce) can evaporated skim milk**
> **½ teaspoon dry mustard**
> **¼ teaspoon ground nutmeg**
> **8 ounces sharp white cheddar cheese, shredded**
> **Salt and freshly ground black pepper**

Cook the macaroni according to the package directions and drain.

Meanwhile, in a large saucepan, whisk together the milk, dry mustard, and nutmeg. Set the pan over medium heat and, when tiny bubbles appear around the edges of the pan, gradually stir in the cheese. Simmer until the cheese melts and the mixture is smooth, stirring constantly. Fold in the cooked macaroni. Remove the pan from the heat and season to taste with salt and pepper.

Serve, or refrigerate the mac 'n' cheese until ready to reheat and either serve or pack in an insulated container for lunch.

Penne with Tomatoes, Basil & Cubed Mozzarella

Serves 4 ■ Prep time: 20 to 25 minutes

Think of this meal as a beefed-up Caprese salad. I turned the classic Italian appetizer into a main dish by combining tomatoes, mozzarella, and fresh basil with tender penne pasta. The hint of oregano and good-quality olive oil round out the dish. This is truly an ideal meal for finicky palates.

This dish can be made up to 24 hours in advance and refrigerated until ready to serve or pack for lunch.

1 pound penne

1 (14-ounce) can diced tomatoes, undrained (regular or fire-roasted)

¼ cup chopped fresh basil

1 tablespoon olive oil

1 teaspoon dried oregano

Salt and freshly ground black pepper

8 ounces part-skim mozzarella or fresh mozzarella cheese, cut into ½-inch cubes

Cook the penne according to the package directions. Drain and transfer to a large bowl. Add the tomatoes, basil, oil, and oregano and toss to combine. Season to taste with salt and pepper.

When the pasta has cooled slightly, fold in the cheese. Serve, or refrigerate until ready to serve or pack for lunch.

Zucchini-Havarti Panini with Fig Jam

Serves 2 ■ Prep time: 15 minutes ■ Cooking time: 6 to 8 minutes

Havarti is a pale yellow, semisoft cow's milk cheese that works well in this sandwich because its flavor complements the zucchini and fruit jam. Plus, it melts nicely. If you don't want to use the fig jam, substitute orange marmalade or apricot preserves. If you don't have a panini press, you may cook the sandwiches in a large skillet, pressing them down with a heavy pan while cooking. If you're cooking for a larger group, this recipe is easily doubled to serve four instead of two.

The sandwiches can be assembled up to 24 hours in advance and refrigerated until ready to cook.

Nutrients per serving:
Calories: 303
Fat: 19g
Saturated Fat: 12g
Cholesterol: 51mg
Carbohydrate: 17g
Protein: 16g
Fiber: 2g
Sodium: 464mg

Cooking spray
¼ cup fig jam
4 slices Italian bread (about ½ inch thick) or 2 sub rolls, split
4 slices Havarti cheese (about 8 ounces total)
1 medium zucchini, thinly sliced
1 yellow summer squash, thinly sliced

Coat a panini press or large skillet with cooking spray and preheat over medium-high heat.

Spread 1 tablespoon fig jam on each slice of bread or 2 tablespoons inside each sub roll. Top 2 bread slices or each sub roll with 1 slice of the cheese. Top the cheese with the zucchini and yellow squash slices. Place the second slice of bread on top, or close the sub rolls, and transfer the sandwiches to the panini press. Cook the sandwiches according to the manufacturer's instructions. If using a skillet, press the sandwiches down with a heavy pan and cook for 3 to 4 minutes per side, until the bread is golden brown and the cheese melts.

Strawberry-Cucumber Salad with Hazelnuts

Serves 4 ■ Prep time: 10 minutes

Nutrients per serving:
Calories: 113
Fat: 8g
Saturated Fat: 1g
Cholesterol: 0mg
Carbohydrate: 9g
Protein: 2g
Fiber: 3g
Sodium: 2mg

Consider this: sweet and toasty hazelnuts and succulent strawberries enlivened with a little vinegar. Sounds like the perfect salad, right? I concur. When serving this salad as a side dish at home, I like to spoon it into Bibb or butter lettuce leaves.

If you can, make this salad the same day you plan to serve it so that the strawberries don't break down and the nuts stay crisp.

1 English (seedless) cucumber, cut into 1-inch pieces (about 2 cups)
2 cups thinly sliced fresh strawberries
1 tablespoon chopped fresh mint
1 tablespoon sherry vinegar
2 teaspoons olive oil
Salt and freshly ground black pepper
½ cup coarsely chopped hazelnuts

In a medium bowl, combine the cucumber, strawberries, mint, vinegar, and oil. Toss to combine. Season to taste with salt and pepper.

Just before serving, fold in the hazelnuts.

Ham & Swiss Wraps with Apricot Preserves

Serves 2 ■ Prep time: 10 minutes

Salty ham partners perfectly with sweet apricot preserves. I've also made these wraps with orange marmalade. I love the balance of flavors that results from the combination of ham, preserves, cheese, and spinach. You can also make these wraps with smoked turkey or chicken breast. If you want to serve the wraps warm, wrap them in plastic wrap or a paper towel and microwave on HIGH power for 15 to 20 seconds.

To reduce the amount of sodium in the wraps, substitute reduced-sodium Swiss cheese.

The wraps can be made up to 24 hours in advance and refrigerated until ready to serve.

Nutrients per serving:
Calories: 493
Fat: 20g
Saturated Fat: 11g
Cholesterol: 77mg
Carbohydrate: 51g
Protein: 31g
Fiber: 3g
Sodium: 737mg

¼ cup apricot preserves
2 fajita-size flour tortillas (regular or whole wheat)
½ cup baby spinach
4 ounces Swiss cheese, thinly sliced
4 ounces reduced-sodium smoked or baked ham, thinly sliced

Spread the apricot preserves on one side of the tortillas, to within ¼ inch of the edges. Top the preserves with the spinach, cheese, and ham. Roll up the tortillas and serve, or wrap in plastic wrap and refrigerate until ready to serve.

Nut Butter & Fruit Preserve Cracker Sandwiches

Serves 2 ■ Prep time: 10 minutes

I know, I know. Marshmallow Fluff isn't considered a nutritional role model, but let's face it: It's wonderful with nut butters and preserves. These cracker sandwiches might actually get your finicky eater to try something new. Feel free to use your imagination when making them—choose your nut butter and then partner it with your favorite fruit preserve. You can also swap the cracker variety to choose something your whole family will enjoy.

Nutrients per serving:
Calories: 161
Fat: 7g
Saturated Fat: 1g
Cholesterol: 0mg
Carbohydrate: 23g
Protein: 2g
Fiber: 1g
Sodium: 234mg

4 teaspoons nut butter (such as almond butter)
8 whole wheat saltine crackers
4 teaspoons Marshmallow Fluff
4 teaspoons strawberry or raspberry preserves

Spread the nut butter onto one side of 4 of the crackers. Top the nut butter with the Marshmallow Fluff and then with the fruit preserves. Top with the remaining crackers and serve, or wrap in plastic wrap until ready to serve or pack for lunch.

Corn, Tomato & Avocado Salad

Serves 4 ■ Prep time: 10 minutes

I decided to put all my favorite ingredients together, and behold: the most amazing salad ever! Sweet corn and tomato combine with tender avocado, fresh cilantro, and white balsamic vinegar. I often prefer white balsamic vinegar to the darker variety because it's mild and doesn't discolor the other ingredients. When I want to add a little smoky flavor, I add ½ teaspoon ground cumin. If desired, you can make this salad with white corn or a combination of white and yellow corn. For added protein and fiber, include a can of black or pink beans, rinsed and drained.

The corn salad can be made up to 24 hours in advance and refrigerated until ready to serve or pack for lunch.

Nutrients per serving:
Calories: 226
Fat: 11g
Saturated Fat: 2g
Cholesterol: 0mg
Carbohydrate: 34g
Protein: 5g
Fiber: 8g
Sodium: 14mg

1 (16-ounce) package thawed frozen yellow corn
2 cups diced tomato
1 cup diced avocado
¼ cup chopped fresh cilantro
1 tablespoon white balsamic vinegar
2 teaspoons olive oil
Salt and freshly ground black pepper

In a large bowl, combine the corn, tomato, avocado, cilantro, vinegar, and oil. Toss to combine. Season to taste with salt and pepper. Serve, or refrigerate until ready to serve or pack for lunch.

Hummus & Bell Pepper "Sushi" on Lavash

Serves 4 ■ Prep time: 10 to 15 minutes

Lavash is a soft, thin flatbread typically sold in the bakery or deli section of the grocery store. Because it's so soft, it rolls up perfectly to make "sushi." In this recipe, I fill the lavash with creamy hummus, roasted red peppers, spinach, and parsley. It's colorful and complex, yet not so complex that it won't please all family members. If you can't find lavash, use regular thin flatbread.

The lavash roll can be assembled up to 24 hours in advance. Wrap the sliced rounds in plastic wrap and refrigerate until ready to serve or pack for lunch.

Nutrients per serving:
Calories: 230
Fat: 6g
Saturated Fat: 1g
Cholesterol: 0mg
Carbohydrate: 38g
Protein: 10g
Fiber: 7g
Sodium: 672mg

1 lavash flatbread (regular or whole wheat)

½ cup roasted garlic or regular hummus

1 cup thinly sliced roasted red peppers

1 cup baby spinach

¼ cup chopped fresh parsley

Place the lavash on a flat surface. Spread the hummus all over one side of the lavash, to within ¼ inch of the edges. Top the hummus with the roasted red peppers and spinach. Sprinkle the parsley over the peppers and spinach. Starting from a shorter end, roll up the lavash tightly. Using a sharp knife, cut the lavash roll crosswise into 2-inch-thick rounds. Serve, or wrap the rounds in plastic wrap and refrigerate until ready to serve or pack for lunch.

Grilled Portobello & Pesto Pita Pockets

Serves 2 ■ Prep time: 10 minutes ■ Cooking time: 10 minutes

I adore the meatiness of portobello mushrooms. I often prefer grilling the mushroom caps because it brings out their natural earthiness and adds another dimension of flavor. You'll find that they are particularly awesome when partnered with basil pesto, Parmesan cheese, and balsamic vinegar, as they are in this dish.

The pita pockets can be made up to 24 hours in advance and refrigerated until ready to serve or pack for lunch. They don't need to be reheated and can be eaten at room temperature.

Nutrients per serving:

Calories: 284

Fat: 9g

Saturated Fat: 2g

Cholesterol: 6mg

Carbohydrate: 42g

Protein: 11g

Fiber: 7g

Sodium: 508mg

Cooking spray

2 large portobello mushroom caps, stems removed

2 teaspoons balsamic vinegar

Salt and freshly ground black pepper

2 teaspoons grated Parmesan cheese

2 tablespoons prepared basil pesto

2 pita pockets (regular or whole wheat), split open

Coat a stovetop grill pan or large skillet with cooking spray and preheat over medium-high heat.

Brush both sides of the mushroom caps with the balsamic vinegar and season both sides with salt and pepper. Place the mushroom caps on the hot pan and cook for 2 to 3 minutes per side, until the mushrooms are tender and releasing liquid. Arrange the mushrooms stem side up and sprinkle the inside of the caps with the Parmesan. Cook for 1 minute, until the cheese melts into the mushrooms.

Spread the pesto on the inside of the pita pockets. Place the mushrooms inside the pita pockets and serve, or wrap in plastic wrap and refrigerate until ready to serve or pack for lunch.

Mushroom & Spinach Quesadillas

Serves 2 ■ Prep time: 10 minutes ■ Cooking time: 10 to 15 minutes

These quesadillas are super cheesy thanks to a blend of incredibly meltable Monterey Jack and cheddar cheeses. They're also a little smoky, thanks to the hint of cumin. I like to add spinach, but you could add onions and bell peppers instead, if you prefer. If you want to reduce the amount of sodium in the quesadillas, opt for reduced-sodium cheese. If you don't have a large griddle, you can cook the quesadillas, one at a time, in a large skillet.

The quesadillas can be made up to 24 hours in advance and refrigerated until ready to serve or pack for lunch. They don't need to be reheated and can be eaten at room temperature.

Nutrients per serving:
Calories: 455
Fat: 23g
Saturated Fat: 13g
Cholesterol: 50mg
Carbohydrate: 41g
Protein: 20g
Fiber: 4g
Sodium: 852mg

Cooking spray
2 cups thinly sliced cremini mushrooms
2 cups baby spinach
½ teaspoon ground cumin
Salt and freshly ground black pepper
4 fajita-size flour tortillas (regular or whole wheat)
1 cup shredded Mexican cheese blend

Coat a large skillet with cooking spray and preheat over medium-high heat. Add the mushrooms to the skillet and cook for 3 minutes, until the mushrooms are tender and releasing liquid. Add the spinach and cumin and cook for 30 seconds, or until the spinach wilts. Remove the pan from the heat and stir in ¼ teaspoon each of salt and pepper.

Coat a large griddle with cooking spray and preheat over medium-high heat.

Arrange 2 of the tortillas on a flat surface. Top the tortillas with the cheese and then with the mushroom mixture. Top the filling with the remaining tortillas. Place the quesadillas in the hot skillet and cook for 2 to 3 minutes per side, until the quesadillas are golden brown on both sides and the cheese melts. Cut the quesadillas into wedges and serve, or wrap in plastic wrap and refrigerate until ready to serve or pack for lunch.

Lemony Sweet Pea Risotto

Serves 4 ■ Prep time: 25 to 30 minutes

Sweet peas and tart lemon create a match made in culinary heaven. In this dish, I partner the two and then add mildly garlicky shallots. As the starchy Arborio rice absorbs the flavor of the shallots and chicken broth, frequent stirring creates a smooth consistency and rich sauce.

The risotto can be made up to 24 hours in advance and refrigerated until ready to reheat and serve or pack in an insulated container for lunch. It may also be eaten at room temperature.

Nutrients per serving:
Calories: 173
Fat: 4g
Saturated Fat: 1g
Cholesterol: 0mg
Carbohydrate: 27g
Protein: 8g
Fiber: 2g
Sodium: 148mg

2 teaspoons olive oil
¼ cup finely diced shallots
1 cup Arborio rice
4 to 5 cups reduced-sodium chicken broth
Zest and juice of 1 lemon
1 cup frozen petite peas
Salt and freshly ground black pepper

Heat the oil in a large saucepan over medium heat. Add the shallots and cook for 3 minutes, or until tender. Add the rice and cook for 3 minutes, stirring frequently, until the rice becomes translucent. Add ½ cup of the chicken broth and stir until the broth is absorbed. Add another ½ cup broth and cook until the liquid is absorbed. Continue adding the broth, ½ cup at a time (add the next ½ cup once the liquid from the previous ½ cup is absorbed), for 15 to 20 minutes, until the rice is tender and the mixture is creamy, stirring frequently.

Stir in 1 tablespoon of the lemon juice and 1 teaspoon of the lemon zest. Fold in the frozen peas and cook until the peas are crisp-tender, about 1 minute, adding more broth if necessary.

Season to taste with salt and pepper. Serve, or refrigerate until ready to reheat and either serve or pack in an insulated container for lunch.

Quinoa Salad with Black Beans, Corn & Cilantro

Serves 4 ■ Prep time: 25 minutes

Quinoa is a protein-packed food that cooks up almost translucent and delivers a subtle nutty flavor (we treat it as a whole grain, though technically we are eating the seeds of the plant). It's an excellent base for this Mexican-inspired salad that's brimming with black beans, corn, cilantro, and lime. When I want a little smoky flavor, I add about 1 teaspoon ground cumin, ground chipotle chile powder, or smoked paprika.

The quinoa salad can be made up to 24 hours in advance and refrigerated until ready to serve or pack for lunch. It can be eaten chilled or at room temperature.

Nutrients per serving:
Calories: 271
Fat: 6g
Saturated Fat: 1g
Cholesterol: 0mg
Carbohydrate: 48g
Protein: 11g
Fiber: 8g
Sodium: 178mg

1 cup quinoa
1 (15-ounce) can black beans, rinsed and drained
1 cup thawed frozen white corn
¼ cup chopped fresh cilantro
Zest and juice of 1 lime
1 tablespoon olive oil
Salt and freshly ground black pepper

Cook the quinoa according to the package directions. Drain and transfer to a large bowl.

Add the black beans, corn, cilantro, 1 tablespoon of the lime juice, 1 teaspoon of the lime zest, and olive oil and toss to combine. Season to taste with salt and pepper. Serve, or refrigerate until ready to serve or pack for lunch.

French Bread Pizza with Mozzarella & Parmesan

Serves 2 ■ Prep time: 5 to 10 minutes ■ Cooking time: 2 to 3 minutes

Nutrients per serving:
Calories: 293
Fat: 8g
Saturated Fat: 4g
Cholesterol: 17mg
Carbohydrate: 40g
Protein: 16g
Fiber: 2g
Sodium: 664mg

Everyone loves French bread pizzas. They're super easy to prepare, and the crusty bread is the perfect base for tomato sauce, mozzarella and Parmesan cheeses, and fresh basil. You can also top the pizzas with turkey or soy pepperoni or diced ham. I recommend putting the meat directly on the sauce, under the cheese layer, so that it doesn't burn under the broiler.

You can assemble and cook these pizzas a few hours in advance; I don't recommend making them the night before because the bread will get soggy. Wrap them in plastic wrap and keep at room temperature until ready to serve.

1 (4-inch-long) piece French bread, halved lengthwise
¼ cup prepared pasta or pizza sauce of your choice
½ cup shredded part-skim mozzarella cheese
2 teaspoons grated Parmesan cheese
1 tablespoon chopped fresh basil

Preheat the broiler and line a baking sheet with aluminum foil.

Arrange the French bread halves on the baking sheet. Top each bread half with the sauce, mozzarella, and then the Parmesan. Place the baking sheet under the broiler and broil for 2 to 3 minutes, until the cheese melts.

Remove the pizzas from the oven and top with the basil. Serve, or let cool slightly and wrap in plastic wrap until ready to serve or pack for lunch.

Vegetable Platter with Tahini-Lemon Yogurt Dip
Apple Salad with Cubed Cheddar & Pecans
Brie & Green Apple Flatbread with Toasted Almonds
Bruschetta with Herbed Cheese & Sliced Peaches
Cucumber Boats with Herbed Ricotta & Parmesan
Mixed-Cereal Granola with Carob Chips
Figs Stuffed with Cream Cheese & Raisins
Baked Kale Chips with Sea Salt
Baked Goat Cheese with Pistachios
Frozen Watermelon & Yogurt Triangles
Frozen Vanilla–Mango Bars
Roasted Corn Guacamole with Baked Tortilla Chips
Warm Spinach Dip with Sun-Dried Tomatoes & Pepper Jack
Coconut-Pineapple Smoothie
Peanut Butter–Chocolate Shake
Kiwi-Honeydew Smoothie
Crackers & Cheese with Strawberry-Grape Salsa
Cheddar Baked Snack Mix
Cottage Cheese & Feta–Smeared Crackers with Sliced Strawberries
Cranberry-Almond Snack Mix
Eggplant Caponata with Melba Toast Crackers

CHAPTER 3

After-School Snacks
(for Parents *and* Kids!)

Vegetable Platter with Tahini-Lemon Yogurt Dip

Serves 4 ■ Prep time: 10 minutes

I frequently put fresh vegetables out when we get home from school. I want my boys to enjoy a snack but I never want to ruin their appetites for dinner. A healthy dip on the side is always a welcome addition. This lemony, sesame-infused dip works with any and all vegetables. Put out an assortment and let the noshing begin!

The dip can be made up to 3 days in advance and refrigerated until ready to serve. For larger groups, simply double or triple the recipe.

6 ounces low-fat plain yogurt

2 tablespoons tahini (sesame paste)

Juice and zest of 1 lemon

½ teaspoon ground cumin

Assortment of vegetables (carrots, celery, zucchini, yellow squash, cherry tomatoes, broccoli, cauliflower, jicama, and/or green beans)

In a medium bowl, whisk together the yogurt, tahini, 2 teaspoons of the lemon juice, 1 teaspoon of the lemon zest, and the cumin.

Serve the dip with an assortment of vegetables on the side.

Apple Salad with Cubed Cheddar & Pecans

Serves 4 ■ Prep time: 10 to 15 minutes

I like to use McIntosh apples for this salad because they have a nice balance between sweet and tart, a flavor profile that partners well with pecans, cheddar cheese, lemon, and parsley. In fact, the mixture is so perfectly balanced that it makes a great topping for grilled or roasted chicken or pork. You may also use Fuji, Gala, Granny Smith, Red Delicious, or your favorite apple variety. When you're ready for a change, make this salad with walnuts and pears and add dried cranberries or dried cherries.

Nutrients per serving:
Calories: 260
Fat: 16g
Saturated Fat: 4g
Cholesterol: 15mg
Carbohydrate: 28g
Protein: 5g
Fiber: 6g
Sodium: 94mg

½ cup chopped pecans
4 McIntosh apples, cored and cut into 2-inch pieces
1 cup cubed sharp cheddar cheese
Juice and zest of 1 lemon
2 tablespoons chopped fresh parsley

Place the pecans in a small dry skillet and set the pan over medium heat. Cook for 3 to 5 minutes, shaking the pan frequently, until the pecans are toasted. Remove the pecans from the heat.

In a large bowl, combine the apples, cheese, 1 tablespoon of the lemon juice, 1 teaspoon of the lemon zest, and the parsley. Toss to combine. Fold in the pecans.

Brie & Green Apple Flatbread with Toasted Almonds

Serves 4 ■ Prep time: 10 to 15 minutes

Nutrients per serving:
Calories: 328
Fat: 14g
Saturated Fat: 6g
Cholesterol: 28mg
Carbohydrate: 42g
Protein: 13g
Fiber: 6g
Sodium: 484mg

The inspiration for this dish came from one of my favorite holiday appetizers, Brie en croute, which is a pastry-wrapped wheel of Brie that's baked until golden brown. I love it served with apples and almonds. Instead of waiting for the holiday season, you can enjoy those same flavors any day of the week. And, for variety, substitute any spreadable cheese for the Brie, including a mild goat cheese or herbed cheese, and top the cheese with any fruit and nut combination.

For a gluten-free version, use your favorite gluten-free bread and roll it out with a rolling pin to flatten it. For larger groups, simply double or triple the recipe.

- ¼ **cup slivered blanched almonds**
- 4 **ounces Brie cheese, at room temperature**
- 1 **flatbread (regular, whole wheat, or seasoned)**
- 2 **Granny Smith apples, cored and thinly sliced**

Place the almonds in a small dry skillet and set the pan over medium heat. Cook for 3 to 5 minutes, shaking the pan frequently, until the almonds are toasted. Remove the almonds from the heat.

Spread the Brie all over the flatbread, to within ¼ inch of the edges. Top the Brie with the apple slices and toasted almonds. Cut the flatbread into squares and serve.

Bruschetta with Herbed Cheese & Sliced Peaches

Serves 4 ■ Prep time: 15 minutes

Herbed cheese is a soft, spreadable cheese loaded with fresh and dried herbs. Because it's mildly salty, it comes to life when served with something sweet, like peaches. If fresh peaches (or nectarines) aren't in season, use thawed frozen peaches (pat them dry before using) or sliced pears.

If you're short on time, instead of toasting the bread, use the toast squares sold in the cracker aisle, cheese department, or deli section of the grocery store. For larger groups, simply double or triple the recipe.

1 small loaf Italian bread, cut crosswise into ½-inch-thick slices

4 ounces herbed cheese (such as Boursin or Alouette)

2 ripe peaches, pitted and thinly sliced

Preheat the oven to 375°F.

Arrange the bread slices on a large baking sheet and bake for 5 to 7 minutes, until golden brown and toasted.

Spread the cheese all over the toasted bread. Arrange the peach slices on top.

Nutrients per serving:

Calories: 274

Fat: 10g

Saturated Fat: 6g

Cholesterol: 25mg

Carbohydrate: 38g

Protein: 8g

Fiber: 3g

Sodium: 524mg

Cucumber Boats with Herbed Ricotta & Parmesan

Serves 4 ■ Prep time: 10 minutes

I like to keep a big batch of this Parmesan- and herb-spiked ricotta filling in the refrigerator, not only for this recipe but also to use as a bagel and sandwich spread and a dip for baby carrots and celery sticks. You can add anything you want to the ricotta mixture. I like to add capers, pickle relish, diced pimento-stuffed olives, diced roasted red peppers, and diced oil-packed sun-dried tomatoes.

You can prepare the ricotta filling up to 3 days in advance and refrigerate until ready to spoon into the cucumber boats. The boats can be assembled up to 24 hours in advance and refrigerated until ready to serve.

Nutrients per serving:
Calories: 105
Fat: 6g
Saturated Fat: 3.5g
Cholesterol: 21mg
Carbohydrate: 5g
Protein: 8g
Fiber: 1g
Sodium: 117mg

- **1 English (seedless) cucumber, halved lengthwise**
- **1 cup part-skim ricotta cheese**
- **2 tablespoons grated Parmesan cheese**
- **2 teaspoons salt-free Italian seasoning**
- **Salt and freshly ground black pepper**

Using a small spoon, scoop out the tiny (edible) seeds from each cucumber half, making canoe-like boats. Halve each cucumber crosswise, making 4 boats.

In a small bowl, whisk together the ricotta, Parmesan, and Italian seasoning. Season to taste with salt and pepper. Spoon the mixture into the cucumber boats.

Mixed-Cereal Granola with Carob Chips

Serves 6 ■ Prep time: 10 minutes ■ Cooking time: 30 minutes

I grew up eating carob chips, a chocolate-like confection that's slightly more bitter than regular chocolate. The flavor pairs perfectly with sweet honey. For a hint of cinnamon, add ½ teaspoon ground cinnamon to the mixture just before baking. You can also add dried fruit to this recipe—I love dried cranberries, cherries, blueberries, mango, and/or raisins.

The granola can be made up to 4 days in advance and stored in an airtight container at room temperature.

Nutrients per serving:
Calories: 279
Fat: 11g
Saturated Fat: 4.5g
Cholesterol: 0mg
Carbohydrate: 43g
Protein: 4g
Fiber: 3g
Sodium: 42mg

Cooking spray
1 cup rolled oats (not instant)
1 cup whole grain O-shaped cereal
½ cup slivered blanched almonds
¼ cup honey
2 teaspoons canola oil
½ cup carob chips

Preheat the oven to 300°F. Coat a large baking sheet with cooking spray.

In a large bowl, combine the oats, cereal, and almonds.

In a small bowl, whisk together the honey and oil. Add the honey mixture to the oat mixture and toss to coat. Spread the mixture out on the prepared baking sheet.

Bake for 30 minutes, stirring every 10 minutes, until the mixture is toasted and golden brown. Let cool slightly before stirring in the carob chips.

Figs Stuffed with Cream Cheese & Raisins

Serves 4 ■ Prep time: 10 minutes

You'll adore this unique snack because I add balsamic vinegar to the fig filling. The tanginess of the vinegar is the perfect complement for the sweet figs and raisins. I also chose strawberry cream cheese because strawberries and balsamic vinegar have a natural affinity. You may use plain cream cheese, if desired.

8 dried figs

4 ounces light strawberry cream cheese, softened

2 tablespoons raisins

1 teaspoon balsamic vinegar

Slice off the stem end of each fig and, using a small spoon, scoop out the center.

In a small bowl, combine the cream cheese, raisins, and vinegar. Mix until well blended. Spoon the cream cheese mixture into the figs and serve.

Nutrients per serving:
Calories: 125
Fat: 4g
Saturated Fat: 2g
Cholesterol: 13mg
Carbohydrate: 22g
Protein: 3g
Fiber: 2g
Sodium: 109mg

Baked Kale Chips with Sea Salt

Serves 4 ■ Prep time: 10 minutes ■ Cooking time: 12 to 15 minutes

This is a colorful and fun alternative to regular potato chips (and a great way to get your kids to try kale for the first time). Kale chips are crunchy, salty, and crammed with nutrients like vitamin C, folate, and fiber. I prefer using sea salt for its crunchy and distinct addition to these chips, but you can use kosher salt instead if that's what you have on hand.

1 bunch kale, rinsed and patted dry

2 teaspoons olive oil

½ teaspoon sea salt (preferably coarse sea salt)

Nutrients per serving:

Calories: 54

Fat: 3g

Saturated Fat: <1g

Cholesterol: 0mg

Carbohydrate: 7g

Protein: 2g

Fiber: 1g

Sodium: 269mg

Preheat the oven to 350°F.

Cut the leaves away from the thick kale stems and rip the leaves into bite-size pieces.

Place the kale in a large bowl, add the olive oil, and toss to coat the leaves. Arrange the kale on a large baking sheet in a single layer, and sprinkle with the sea salt. Bake for 12 to 15 minutes, until the kale leaves are crisp and golden brown around the edges.

Baked Goat Cheese with Pistachios

Serves 4 ■ Prep time: 5 to 10 minutes ■ Cooking time: 8 to 10 minutes

I spruced up regular goat cheese in this recipe by adding fresh chives and dried oregano. Sweet and nutty pistachios add flavor and crunch to the warm, spreadable dip. For larger parties, simply double or triple the recipe and place the ramekins in different places around your home (dining room, kitchen, patio, and so forth).

For a gluten-free version, serve the warm goat cheese with fresh vegetables on the side instead of pretzels.

6 ounces soft goat cheese (regular or with herbs)
1 tablespoon minced fresh chives
½ teaspoon dried oregano
¼ cup chopped pistachios
2 cups mini pretzel twists

Preheat the oven to 350°F.

In a small bowl, combine the goat cheese, chives, and oregano. Mix until well blended. Spoon the mixture into a 6 or 8-inch ramekin and top with the pistachios. Bake for 8 to 10 minutes, until the goat cheese is golden brown on top.

Serve the goat cheese with the pretzels on the side.

Nutrients per serving:
Calories: 181
Fat: 13g
Saturated Fat: 7g
Cholesterol: 20mg
Carbohydrate: 8g
Protein: 10g
Fiber: 1g
Sodium: 253mg

Frozen Watermelon & Yogurt Triangles

Serves 4 ■ Prep time: 5 minutes ■ Freezing time: 1 hour

It's wise to keep healthy treats in the freezer for last-minute snacks on hot afternoons. In this recipe, I embellished vanilla yogurt with confectioners' sugar and vanilla extract to create a wonderful coating for watermelon. You may also use slices of cantaloupe and honeydew melon.

The watermelon triangles can be prepared up to 1 week in advance and frozen until ready to serve. For larger groups, simply double or triple the recipe.

8 ounces low-fat vanilla yogurt

2 tablespoons confectioners' sugar

½ teaspoon vanilla extract

8 (1-inch-thick) triangles of watermelon, 4 to 6 inches long

In a shallow dish, whisk together the yogurt, confectioners' sugar, and vanilla. Dip the watermelon triangles into the yogurt mixture, coating about two-thirds of the flesh. Transfer the watermelon to a large baking sheet and freeze until the yogurt is firm, about 1 hour.

Nutrients per serving:

Calories: 107

Fat: 1g

Saturated Fat: <1g

Cholesterol: 4mg

Carbohydrate: 23g

Protein: 3g

Fiber: 1g

Sodium: 32mg

Frozen Vanilla-Mango Bars

Serves 4 ■ Prep time: 5 to 10 minutes ■ Freezing time: 1 hour

Nutrients per serving:
Calories: 145
Fat: 1g
Saturated Fat: 1g
Cholesterol: 8mg
Carbohydrate: 30g
Protein: 4g
Fiber: 2g
Sodium: 62mg

It's a shame mango has a limited season, because it's so succulent and sweet and it makes an excellent snack and dessert choice. Thankfully, you can also find cubed mango in the freezer aisle. In these bars, I couple the sweetness of mango with the tanginess of vanilla yogurt. It's so simple, yet so creamy and sweet. If you don't have ice-pop molds, pour the mixture into small plastic cups, insert a plastic spoon or wooden craft stick, and freeze until firm.

The bars can be made up to 4 days in advance and frozen until ready to serve. For larger groups, simply double or triple the recipe.

2 cups low-fat vanilla yogurt
2 cups cubed mango
½ teaspoon vanilla extract

Combine all of the ingredients in a blender and puree until smooth. Pour the mixture into four ice-pop molds (about ½ cup in volume) and freeze until firm, about 1 hour.

Roasted Corn Guacamole with Baked Tortilla Chips

Serves 4 ■ Prep time: 5 to 10 minutes ■ Cooking time: 15 minutes

I made this chunky guacamole extra special by adding sweet roasted corn, ground cumin, and fresh cilantro. For more zing, add 1 tablespoon fresh lime juice and 1 teaspoon finely grated lime zest. You can also make the guacamole heartier by adding grilled or roasted chicken, grilled or steamed shrimp, or rinsed and drained canned black beans.

Nutrients per serving:
Calories: 281
Fat: 10g
Saturated Fat: 1g
Cholesterol: 0mg
Carbohydrate: 47g
Protein: 7g
Fiber: 7g
Sodium: 128mg

Cooking spray
2 cups thawed frozen yellow corn
1 teaspoon ground cumin
Salt and freshly ground black pepper
1 ripe avocado, pitted, peeled, and diced
¼ cup chopped fresh cilantro
4 cups baked corn tortilla chips

Preheat the oven to 400°F. Coat a large baking sheet with cooking spray.

In a large bowl, combine the corn, cumin, ½ teaspoon salt, and ¼ teaspoon pepper. Toss to coat the corn. Transfer the corn to the prepared baking sheet and bake for 15 minutes, or until the corn is golden brown.

Transfer the corn to a large bowl and stir in the avocado and cilantro. Serve warm, at room temperature, or chilled, with the tortilla chips on the side.

Warm Spinach Dip with Sun-Dried Tomatoes & Pepper Jack

Serves 4 ■ Prep time: 10 minutes ■ Cooking time: 15 minutes

Nutrients per serving:
Calories: 286
Fat: 20g
Saturated Fat: 11g
Cholesterol: 60mg
Carbohydrate: 14g
Protein: 12g
Fiber: 2g
Sodium: 376mg

Spinach dip is a quintessential staple at most parties. Notice the word essential nestled in that word: The dip is downright mandatory in some circles. Not surprising, considering it's smooth and creamy and hits your palate from all angles. My version boasts hints of onion, sun-dried tomatoes, and pepper Jack cheese, making it truly unique. If you don't want the mildly hot peppers in your dip, substitute regular Monterey Jack cheese for the pepper Jack. I typically serve this dip with pita triangles, bagel chips, whole grain crackers, or vegetables.

The dip can be made up to 24 hours in advance and refrigerated until ready to bake.

16 ounces frozen chopped spinach, thawed and well drained (squeeze in paper towels to remove all liquid)

1½ cups light sour cream

1 cup shredded pepper Jack cheese

½ cup diced oil-packed sun-dried tomatoes

¼ cup grated red onion

Preheat the oven to 350°F.

In a large bowl, combine the spinach, sour cream, cheese, sun-dried tomatoes, and onion. Mix well to combine.

Transfer the mixture to a small baking dish (6 to 8 inches in diameter) and bake for 15 minutes, or until the top is golden brown and the dip is bubbly. Serve hot or warm.

Coconut-Pineapple Smoothie

Serves 4 ■ Prep time: 5 to 10 minutes

Get ready for the Hawaiian breeze that comes with this scrumptious beverage. Few things rival the combination of pineapple and coconut. When I have extra time and ingredients, I love to garnish this smoothie with dried banana chips—they add flavor and crunch (look for them in the produce department of the grocery store). For added flair, garnish the rim of the glass with toasted coconut. And for a fun dessert, pour the smoothie into ice-pop molds and freeze until firm. For larger groups, simply double or triple the recipe.

1 (14-ounce) can coconut milk

1 cup diced pineapple (fresh or canned in 100% juice)

1 small banana, peeled

1 cup ice cubes

¼ cup dried banana chips

In a blender, combine the coconut milk, pineapple, banana, and ice cubes. Puree until smooth. Pour the smoothie into tall glasses and top with banana chips.

Nutrients per serving:
Calories: 268
Fat: 24g
Saturated Fat: 21g
Cholesterol: 0mg
Carbohydrate: 17g
Protein: 3g
Fiber: 3g
Sodium: 14mg

Peanut Butter–Chocolate Shake

Serves 1 ■ Prep time: 5 to 10 minutes

This shake is my son Kyle's favorite. It's a magical blend of peanut butter, chocolate, and banana. Kyle decided that 3 ice cubes create the perfect consistency: 2 is not enough and 4 is too many. Feel free to adjust the ingredients to suit your preferences, with more or less peanut butter and/or more or less chocolate syrup. For larger groups, simply double or triple the recipe.

1 small banana, peeled

1 cup low-fat vanilla yogurt

1 tablespoon creamy peanut butter

1 tablespoon chocolate syrup

½ teaspoon vanilla extract

3 ice cubes

Combine all of the ingredients in a blender and puree until smooth. Pour the mixture into a tall glass.

Nutrients per serving:
Calories: 402
Fat: 10g
Saturated Fat: 3g
Cholesterol: 15mg
Carbohydrate: 66g
Protein: 13g
Fiber: 3g
Sodium: 207mg

Kiwi-Honeydew Smoothie

Serves 1 ■ Prep time: 5 to 10 minutes

Because honeydew melon and kiwi are super sweet, I often partner them with tart lemon and yogurt when making smoothies. I add honey to round out the flavor and bring out more sweetness from the fruit. You can also make this smoothie with cantaloupe melon instead of the honeydew. For larger groups, simply double or triple the recipe.

1 cup low-fat vanilla yogurt
1 kiwi, peeled and chopped
1 cup cubed honeydew melon
1 tablespoon honey
Zest and juice of 1 lemon
3 ice cubes

In a blender, combine the yogurt, kiwi, melon, honey, 1 tablespoon of the lemon juice, 1 teaspoon of the lemon zest, and the ice cubes. Puree until smooth. Pour the mixture into a tall glass.

Nutrients per serving:
Calories: 358
Fat: 3g
Saturated Fat: 2g
Cholesterol: 15mg
Carbohydrate: 78g
Protein: 10g
Fiber: 4g
Sodium: 155mg

Crackers & Cheese with Strawberry-Grape Salsa

Serves 2 ■ Prep time: 5 to 10 minutes

Grapes shouldn't be relegated to the snack tray simply as is, because they lend incredible flavor, texture, and variety when incorporated into other dishes. I love this medley of sweet grapes and strawberries in balsamic vinegar because it's served with Swiss cheese and crunchy crackers. Everything comes together perfectly on the plate. You can also top the crackers with toasted slivered almonds just before serving. For a gluten-free version, select your favorite gluten-free cracker, or toast gluten-free bread slices and cut them into squares.

The salsa can be made up to 24 hours in advance and refrigerated until ready to serve.

Nutrients per serving:
Calories: 314
Fat: 18g
Saturated Fat: 11g
Cholesterol: 52mg
Carbohydrate: 21g
Protein: 17g
Fiber: 2g
Sodium: 206mg

½ cup chopped fresh strawberries
½ cup diced green grapes
1 teaspoon white balsamic vinegar
4 ounces Jarlsberg or Swiss cheese, thinly sliced
12 whole grain crackers

In a medium bowl, combine the strawberries, grapes, and vinegar. Mix to combine.

Arrange the cheese on top of the crackers and top the cheese with the salsa.

Cheddar Baked Snack Mix

Serves 4 ■ Prep time: 10 minutes ■ Cooking time: 15 minutes

I realize I'm a chef and cookbook author, but, truth be told, I love the cheddar cheese powder sold in the popcorn aisle (and sometimes in the spice aisle, next to the butter sprinkles). The cheddar flavor is amazing, and a little goes a long way. Once I discovered it for popcorn, I felt compelled to create an alternative use for it. Cheddar isn't the only flavored powder available, so for variety also try the nacho cheddar, ranch, Parmesan and garlic, sour cream and onion, barbecue, salt and vinegar, pizza, and buffalo wing. Enjoy a different snack mix every week!

The snack mix can be made up to 4 days in advance and stored in an airtight container at room temperature. For larger groups, simply double or triple the recipe.

Nutrients per serving:
Calories: 196
Fat: 5g
Saturated Fat: 1g
Cholesterol: 0mg
Carbohydrate: 34g
Protein: 4g
Fiber: 2g
Sodium: 517mg

Cooking spray
1 cup unsalted mini pretzel twists
1 cup rice cereal squares
1 cup corn cereal squares
4 slices pumpernickel bread, cut into 2-inch pieces
1 tablespoon canola oil
2 tablespoons white cheddar cheese powder

Preheat the oven to 300°F. Coat a large baking sheet with cooking spray.

In a large bowl, combine the pretzels, both cereal squares, and pumpernickel bread. Add the canola oil and toss to coat. Add the cheese powder and toss to coat everything with the powder.

Spread the mixture out on the prepared baking sheet in a single layer (use two baking sheets if necessary).

Bake for 15 minutes, stirring halfway through cooking, until the mixture is golden brown.

Cottage Cheese & Feta-Smeared Crackers with Sliced Strawberries

Serves 2 ■ Prep time: 10 minutes

Nutrients per serving:
Calories: 201
Fat: 8g
Saturated Fat: 4g
Cholesterol: 21mg
Carbohydrate: 15g
Protein: 18g
Fiber: 2g
Sodium: 320mg

Cottage cheese is nice by itself, but when you add feta cheese, the flavors soar. Salty feta also pairs very well with sweet strawberries. For a smoother spread, use a food processor to blend the cottage cheese with the feta and oregano. Finicky eaters often prefer cottage cheese that's spiked with pineapple (the flavors also pair very well with the feta cheese and oregano). You may top the crackers with sliced peaches, blackberries, blueberries, or raspberries instead of the strawberries.

You can make the cottage cheese mixture up to 24 hours in advance and refrigerate until ready to serve.

1 cup low-fat, low-sodium cottage cheese
¼ cup crumbled feta cheese
½ teaspoon dried oregano
12 whole grain crackers
½ cup thinly sliced fresh strawberries

In a small bowl, combine the cottage cheese, feta, and oregano. Using a fork, mash the mixture together until well blended. Spread the cottage cheese mixture on the crackers and top with the sliced strawberries.

Cranberry-Almond Snack Mix

Serves 8 ■ Prep time: 5 minutes ■ Cooking time: 8 to 10 minutes

Nutrients per serving:
Calories: 302
Fat: 19g
Saturated Fat: 1g
Cholesterol: 0mg
Carbohydrate: 30g
Protein: 8g
Fiber: 6g
Sodium: 1mg

Almonds and cranberries are wonderful together when you just leave them alone, but when you add cinnamon and toast the almonds, the combination becomes brilliant. Feel free to add and/or substitute your favorite dried fruits and nuts; cherries and walnuts make great choices too. You can also add a handful of mini chocolate chips.

The snack mix can be made up to 4 days in advance and stored in an airtight container at room temperature. For larger groups, simply double or triple the recipe.

Cooking spray
2 cups whole blanched almonds
1 teaspoon ground cinnamon
1 teaspoon canola oil
2 cups dried cranberries

Preheat the oven to 300°F. Coat a large baking sheet with cooking spray.

In a medium bowl, combine the almonds, cinnamon, and canola oil. Toss to coat the almonds with the cinnamon. Spread the almonds out on the prepared baking sheet and bake for 8 to 10 minutes, until the almonds are lightly toasted. Transfer the almonds to a bowl, add the cranberries, and toss to combine.

Eggplant Caponata with Melba Toast Crackers

Serves 4 ■ Prep time: 10 minutes ■ Cooking time: 10 minutes

Traditional caponata boasts both sweet and savory elements from eggplant, onions, vinegar, and other ingredients. I found a way to capture all its glory with just a handful of ingredients (by choosing the right ones). This eggplant mixture is alive with flavor and color, thanks to the perfect pairing of eggplant, olives, and capers, making it not only a super dip but also a great topping for chicken, pork, or steak. For a gluten-free version, substitute your favorite gluten-free bread or crackers for the melba toast.

The caponata can be made up to 24 hours in advance and refrigerated until ready to serve.

Nutrients per serving:
Calories: 142
Fat: 4g
Saturated Fat: <1g
Cholesterol: 0mg
Carbohydrate: 24g
Protein: 3g
Fiber: 4g
Sodium: 486mg

2 teaspoons olive oil

2 cups cubed eggplant (peeled or unpeeled), about 6 ounces

1 (14-ounce) can diced tomatoes with green pepper, celery, and onion, undrained

¼ cup sliced pitted Greek olives

2 teaspoons drained capers

24 melba toast crackers

Heat the oil in a large skillet over medium-high heat. Add the eggplant and cook for 3 minutes, stirring frequently, until golden brown. Add the tomatoes, olives, and capers and bring to a simmer. Decrease the heat to low and simmer for 5 minutes, or until the mixture thickens and the liquid reduces. Serve the caponata warm, at room temperature, or chilled, with the crackers on the side.

PASTA & RISOTTO

Penne with Caramelized Onion & Peaches
Spaghetti–Hot Dog Kebabs
Pasta "Cupcakes" with Mozzarella & Marinara
Toasted Tortellini with Bread Crumbs & Tomato Sauce
Lasagne Rolls with Shredded Chicken & Cheese
Three-Cheese & Eggplant Lasagne
Orzo, Cauliflower & Smoked Gouda Ramekins
Mac 'n' Cheese Croquettes with Tomato Dipping Sauce
Pasta Primavera Salad with White Balsamic Vinaigrette
Green Angel Hair with Black Olive "Eyes"
Ponzu-Spiked Farfalle with Mandarin Oranges
Fusilli with Sun-Dried Tomatoes & Spinach
Singapore Noodles with Vegetables
Wok-Seared Wontons with Baby Corn & Bok Choy
Risotto with Chicken Sausage & Caramelized Onion
Summer Corn Risotto with Parmesan
Herbed Ricotta–Stuffed Shells

CHICKEN & TURKEY

Grilled Chicken Strips with Orange Marmalade Ketchup
Chicken-Fried Chicken with Country-Style
    Buttermilk-Bacon Sauce
Grilled Chicken with Cantaloupe, Cucumber & Lime Salsa
Chicken Pot Pie with Peas & Carrots
Chicken & Chile Cream Cheese Wraps
Orange Chicken with Bok Choy
Parmesan & Pecan–Crusted Chicken
Grilled Chicken with Balsamic Syrup & Crumbled Feta
Chicken Pops with Creamy Barbecue Dip
Chicken Fingers with Peanut Sauce
Baked Chicken with Pears & Red Onion
Chicken Fingers with Almond "Nails"
Chicken Enchiladas with Pepper Jack & Sour Cream
Individual Chicken & Cheese Calzones
Chicken Burgers with Soy-Cilantro Glaze
Shredded Barbecue Chicken with Apple Slaw
Apricot & Lime–Glazed Chicken
Chicken Mozzarella with Buttered Spaghetti
Chicken Sausage & Sweet Onion Pizza
Sun-Dried Tomato Cups with Mexican Chicken
Molasses, Balsamic & Mustard Turkey Tenderloin
Turkey Meatball Sliders
Sweet-and-Sour Turkey Meatballs

SEAFOOD

Shrimp & Tomato Calzone
Cheddar Fondue with Shrimp & Apples
Shrimp & Yellow Squash Skewers
Key West Po'boys with Lime & Mayo
Seared Tilapia with Fresh Fruit Salsa
Tilapia with Tomato-Zucchini Relish
Salt-Baked Salmon with Olive Relish
Grilled Salmon with Ginger–Sweet Onion Vinaigrette
Honey-Pecan Baked Salmon
Salmon-Dill Cakes with Mustard-Yogurt Sauce
Salmon Niçoise with Warm Green Beans, Potatoes
    & Mustard Vinaigrette
Crab Cakes with Creamy Broccoli Slaw
Grilled Tuna with White Peach Salsa
Braised Tuna with Mango, Jicama & Watercress
Seared Tuna with Oranges, Avocado & Cilantro

BEEF

Individual Meat Loaf "Cupcakes" with
    Creamy Ketchup "Icing"
Grilled Steak Lettuce Wraps
Sirloin Kebabs with Bell Peppers & Teriyaki
Roast Beef Chimichangas with Green Chiles & Cheddar
Wok-Seared Beef with Orange & Teriyaki
Grilled Steak Caprese Salad
Grilled Flank Steak with Blackberry Sauce
Southwestern Braised Short Ribs
Sicilian Meatballs

PORK

Roasted Pork Tenderloin with Berry-Almond Salad
Grilled Pork Chops with Sea Salt–Vinegar Slaw
Grilled Pork & Pear Salad with Goat Cheese & Pecans
Wok-Seared Pork with Pineapple, Bell Peppers & Ginger
Pork Chops with Apple Tartar Sauce
Savory Bread Pudding with Ham & Sun-Dried Tomatoes
Mustard-Glazed Ham Steaks with Raspberry Sauce
Cowboy Pizza with Rattlesnake Beans, Bacon & Manchego

VEGETABLE

Spinach Salad with Blueberries, Blue Cheese & Walnuts
White Pizza with Pesto & Asparagus
Eggplant Napoleons with Smoked Mozzarella & Tomato
Spaghetti Squash with Pesto
Roasted Acorn Squash with Spinach & Hazelnuts
Roasted Tomato, Basil & Provolone Panini

CHAPTER 4

Dinner: May I Take Your Order?

Penne with Caramelized Onion & Peaches

Serves 4 ■ Prep time: 5 minutes ■ Cooking time: 20 minutes

This dish balances flavors in a magical way: sweet caramelized onions and peaches with salty feta cheese. I like to use frozen peaches for this recipe because the fruit gets cooked anyway and frozen peaches are already peeled, pitted, and sliced! For a burst of fresh flavor and color, add ¼ cup chopped fresh basil or mint. To make this dish gluten-free, substitute your favorite brand of gluten-free pasta.

1 pound penne

2 teaspoons olive oil

1 cup chopped yellow onion

2 cups peeled and sliced peaches

2 cups reduced-sodium vegetable or chicken broth

Salt and freshly ground black pepper

½ cup crumbled feta cheese (regular or herb seasoned)

Nutrients per serving:
Calories: 543
Fat: 9g
Saturated Fat: 3g
Cholesterol: 17mg
Carbohydrate: 95g
Protein: 18g
Fiber: 4g
Sodium: 281mg

Cook the pasta according to the package directions. Drain and set aside.

Meanwhile, heat the oil in a large skillet over medium heat. Add the onion and cook for 5 to 7 minutes, stirring frequently, until the onion is golden brown and caramelized. Add the peaches and broth and bring to a simmer. Simmer for 5 minutes, or until the liquid reduces slightly.

Add the cooked pasta and cook for 1 minute to heat through. Season to taste with salt and pepper. Transfer the pasta mixture to a serving platter and top with the feta cheese.

Spaghetti–Hot Dog Kebabs

Serves 4 ■ Prep time: 10 to 15 minutes ■ Cooking time: 3 to 5 minutes

My boys love to snack on raw spaghetti, so give it a try! In this recipe, the crisp noodle skewers are fabulous with the smoky hot dogs, sweet bell pepper, and zucchini. Feel free to add a variety of vegetables to the kebabs, such as cherry tomatoes, green bell peppers, yellow squash, and button mushrooms; they all work great. You can also use regular wooden or metal skewers instead of the spaghetti (soak wooden skewers in water for 10 minutes before using to prevent them from burning).

Nutrients per serving:
Calories: 224
Fat: 14g
Saturated Fat: 6g
Cholesterol: 25mg
Carbohydrate: 16g
Protein: 8g
Fiber: 2g
Sodium: 638mg

Cooking spray
4 hot dogs (beef, turkey, or soy), cut crosswise into 1-inch pieces
1 yellow bell pepper, seeded and cut into 1-inch pieces
1 medium zucchini, cut into 1-inch pieces
12 pieces spaghetti (regular, whole wheat, or gluten-free)
Salt and freshly ground black pepper
1 cup pasta sauce of your choice

Coat a stovetop grill pan or griddle with cooking spray and preheat over medium-high heat.

Skewer alternating pieces of the hot dogs, bell pepper, and zucchini onto each piece of spaghetti to make 12 skewers. Season the hot dogs and vegetables with salt and pepper. Brush some of the pasta sauce all over the hot dogs and vegetables. Warm the rest of the sauce in a small saucepan.

Arrange the spaghetti kebabs on the hot pan and cook for 3 to 5 minutes, until the hot dogs are heated through and the vegetables are crisp-tender, turning frequently. Serve the kebabs with the remaining warm pasta sauce on the side for dunking.

Pasta "Cupcakes" with Mozzarella & Marinara

Serves 6 ■ Prep time: 15 minutes ■ Cooking time: 15 to 20 minutes

Think of this dish as macaroni and cheese baked into the shape of a cupcake and served with warm tomato sauce. I love to partner gooey mozzarella cheese with sharp Parmesan, but you can also make the cupcakes with mild or sharp cheddar cheese instead of the mozzarella.

The cupcakes can be assembled up to 24 hours in advance and refrigerated until ready to bake. You can also freeze the assembled cupcakes for up to 3 months. Thaw them completely in the refrigerator before baking. For larger groups, simply double or triple the recipe and fill more muffin cups.

Nutrients per serving:
Calories: 465
Fat: 15g
Saturated Fat: 8g
Cholesterol: 38mg
Carbohydrate: 66g
Protein: 19g
Fiber: 4g
Sodium: 376mg

Cooking spray
1 pound elbow macaroni
2 cups light sour cream
1 cup shredded part-skim mozzarella cheese
2 tablespoons grated Parmesan cheese
Salt and freshly ground black pepper
1 cup marinara sauce of your choice

Preheat the oven to 350°F. Coat a 6-cup muffin pan with cooking spray.

Cook the macaroni according to the package directions. Drain and transfer the macaroni to a large bowl. Add the sour cream, mozzarella, and Parmesan and mix well. Season to taste with salt and pepper.

Spoon the macaroni mixture into the prepared muffin cups. Spoon the pasta sauce over the top.

Bake for 15 to 20 minutes, until the "cupcakes" are hot and the cheese is melted.

Toasted Tortellini with Bread Crumbs & Tomato Sauce

Serves 4 ■ Prep time: 15 minutes ■ Cooking time: 5 minutes

Think of this as an upside-down way to serve your pasta—the sauce goes on the plate first so that you can nestle the golden brown, Parmesan-crusted toasted tortellini on top. It makes for a restaurant-quality presentation.

For birthday parties, arrange the tortellini on top of the sauce on a large serving platter and serve wooden picks on the side. For larger groups, simply double or triple the recipe.

Nutrients per serving:
Calories: 345
Fat: 12g
Saturated Fat: 5g
Cholesterol: 38mg
Carbohydrate: 47g
Protein: 14g
Fiber: 3g
Sodium: 607mg

12 ounces cheese-filled tortellini

1 cup pasta or pizza sauce of your choice

2 teaspoons olive oil

¼ cup reduced-sodium dry bread crumbs

2 tablespoons grated Parmesan cheese

¼ cup chopped fresh basil

Cook the tortellini according to the package directions, and then drain. Heat the pasta sauce in a saucepan.

Heat the oil in a large skillet over medium-high heat. Add the tortellini and cook for 2 minutes, stirring frequently, until golden brown. Add the bread crumbs and Parmesan and toss to coat. Cook for 1 minute to heat through.

Spoon the warm pasta sauce onto individual plates. Arrange the tortellini over the sauce and top with the basil.

Lasagne Rolls with Shredded Chicken & Cheese

Serves 4 ■ Prep time: 15 minutes ■ Cooking time: 30 minutes

This recipe turns an Italian dish into one with Southwest flair. Tender lasagna noodles are filled with a mixture of chicken and ricotta and pepper Jack cheeses, rolled into pinwheels, and nestled over and under prepared salsa before baking. For finicky eaters, you can substitute regular Monterey Jack cheese or a Mexican cheese blend for the pepper Jack. You can also replace the salsa with pasta or pizza sauce.

The rolls can be assembled up to 24 hours in advance and refrigerated until ready to bake. You can also freeze the rolls for up to 3 months. Thaw the rolls completely in the refrigerator before baking. For larger groups, simply double or triple the recipe.

Nutrients per serving:
Calories: 533
Fat: 16g
Saturated Fat: 8g
Cholesterol: 104mg
Carbohydrate: 53g
Protein: 44g
Fiber: 3g
Sodium: 623mg

12 lasagna noodles

1½ cups part-skim ricotta cheese

2 cups finely shredded cooked chicken (poached, grilled, roasted, or rotisserie)

1 cup shredded pepper Jack cheese

1½ cups salsa of your choice

Preheat the oven to 350°F.

Cook the lasagna noodles according to the package directions. Drain and set aside.

Meanwhile, in a large bowl, combine the ricotta, chicken, and pepper Jack cheese. Mix well.

Arrange the lasagna noodles on a flat surface. Spread the chicken mixture onto each noodle in a thin layer (about ½ inch thick). Starting from a shorter end, roll up the lasagna noodles tightly.

Spoon ½ cup of the salsa into the bottom of a shallow baking dish. Spread the salsa out to cover the bottom. Arrange the lasagna rolls (on their sides, with the loose ends facing down) on top of the salsa. Spoon the remaining salsa over the top of the rolls. Cover the dish with aluminum foil and bake for 15 minutes. Uncover and bake for 15 more minutes, or until the cheese melts.

Three-Cheese & Eggplant Lasagne

Serves 4 ■ Prep time: 15 minutes ■ Cooking time: 45 minutes

Nutrients per serving:
Calories: 436
Fat: 24g
Saturated Fat: 15g
Cholesterol: 76mg
Carbohydrate: 22g
Protein: 35g
Fiber: 8g
Sodium: 546mg

This unique, noodle-free lasagne blends sweet and tender eggplant with three cheeses and Italian seasoning. It's eggplant Parmesan meets lasagne. Since eggplant is used instead of noodles, this dish is a perfect gluten-free meal for the entire family. If you want sauce, spoon some warm pasta sauce in the bottom of each dish and arrange the eggplant rolls on top. Garnish with chopped fresh basil.

The lasagne can be assembled up to 24 hours in advance and refrigerated until ready to bake. You can also freeze the lasagne for up to 3 months. Thaw the lasagne completely in the refrigerator before baking.

Cooking spray
2 large eggplant, peeled and sliced lengthwise into ¼-inch-thick strips
Salt and freshly ground black pepper
2 cups part-skim ricotta cheese
2 cups shredded part-skim mozzarella cheese
2 tablespoons grated Parmesan cheese
2 teaspoons salt-free Italian seasoning

Preheat the oven to 350°F. Coat a stovetop griddle, grill pan, or large skillet with cooking spray and preheat over medium-high heat.

Season both sides of the eggplant slices with salt and pepper. Place the eggplant slices on the hot pan and cook for 2 to 3 minutes per side, until golden brown and tender.

Meanwhile, in a large bowl, combine the ricotta, 1 cup of the mozzarella, 1 tablespoon of the Parmesan, and the Italian seasoning. Mix well.

Coat a shallow baking dish with cooking spray. Arrange one-third of the eggplant slices in the bottom of the prepared baking dish. Top with half of the cheese mixture. Arrange half of the remaining eggplant slices over the cheese mixture. Top with the remaining cheese mixture and the remaining eggplant slices. Sprinkle the remaining 1 cup mozzarella and 1 tablespoon Parmesan over the top.

Cover the dish with aluminum foil and bake for 30 minutes. Uncover and bake for 15 more minutes, or until the top is golden brown and bubbly.

Orzo, Cauliflower & Smoked Gouda Ramekins

Serves 6 ■ Prep time: 15 to 20 minutes ■ Cooking time: 20 to 25 minutes

These little baked cups of deliciousness show off rice-shaped orzo pasta, tender cauliflower, smoked cheese, and fresh parsley. The cauliflower tenderizes as it bakes, so there's no need to blanch it first in boiling water. Instead of cauliflower, you can also make this dish with broccoli florets, diced zucchini, frozen corn, or frozen green peas (no need to thaw the frozen vegetables before baking).

The ramekins can be assembled up to 24 hours in advance and refrigerated until ready to bake. You can also freeze the ramekins for up to 3 months. Thaw them completely in the refrigerator before baking.

Cooking spray
1 pound orzo
2 cups light sour cream
2 cups fresh or frozen cauliflower florets (no need to thaw)
1 cup shredded smoked Gouda or smoked mozzarella cheese
¼ cup chopped fresh parsley

Preheat the oven to 350°F. Coat the bottom of 12 ramekins (6 to 8 ounces each) with cooking spray.

Cook the pasta according to the package directions. Drain and transfer the pasta to a large bowl. Fold in the sour cream, cauliflower, Gouda, and parsley. Mix well.

Spoon the pasta mixture into the prepared ramekins. Arrange the ramekins on a large baking sheet and bake for 20 to 25 minutes, until the top is golden brown and the cheese is bubbly.

Mac 'n' Cheese Croquettes with Tomato Dipping Sauce

Serves 4 ■ Prep time: 10 minutes ■ Cooking time: 15 minutes

Nutrients per serving:
Calories: 375
Fat: 5g
Saturated Fat: 2g
Cholesterol: 13mg
Carbohydrate: 65g
Protein: 17g
Fiber: 3g
Sodium: 978mg

This is a unique and fun way to use leftover macaroni and cheese. Buy your favorite brand and prepare extra so you can enjoy making croquettes with the leftovers. You can also make the croquettes with leftover Orzo, Cauliflower & Smoked Gouda Ramekins (page 78). To reduce the sodium in the dish, opt for a reduced-sodium brand of pasta sauce. For larger groups, simply double or triple the recipe.

Cooking spray
4 cups prepared macaroni and cheese, chilled
2 large egg whites
1 cup panko (Japanese bread crumbs)
3 tablespoons grated Parmesan cheese
1 cup pasta or pizza sauce of your choice

Preheat the oven to 350°F. Coat a large baking sheet with cooking spray.

Using wet hands, shape the chilled macaroni and cheese into 4 equal patties, each about 1 inch thick.

Place the egg whites in a shallow dish. Combine the panko and Parmesan in another shallow dish. Dip the patties into the panko mixture and turn to coat. Transfer the patties to the egg whites and turn to coat. Return the patties to the panko mixture and turn to coat both sides.

Transfer the croquettes to the prepared baking sheet and bake for 15 minutes, or until golden brown and heated through. Meanwhile, heat the pasta sauce in a saucepan.

Serve the croquettes with the warm pasta sauce either underneath or drizzled over the top.

Pasta Primavera Salad with White Balsamic Vinaigrette

Serves 4 ■ Prep time: 15 to 20 minutes

Nutrients per serving:
Calories: 470
Fat: 5g
Saturated Fat: 1g
Cholesterol: 0mg
Carbohydrate: 89g
Protein: 16g
Fiber: 4g
Sodium: 869mg

Giardiniera is a fabulous Italian blend of pickled vegetables—typically carrots, cauliflower, celery, and bell peppers. It's available in mild and hot versions, and it's a great addition to any salad. The sweet cherry tomatoes in this recipe balance out the tangy, vinegary flavor. Look for giardiniera in the grocery store alongside the olives, pickles, and roasted red peppers. For added protein, add 8 ounces steamed or grilled shrimp, 2 cups cubed grilled chicken, or 1 cup cubed fresh mozzarella cheese or little mozzarella balls.

The salad can be made up to 3 days in advance and refrigerated until ready to serve.

1 pound penne or fusilli

2 cups giardiniera salad (mild or hot)

1 cup cherry or grape tomatoes, halved

1 tablespoon white balsamic vinegar

1 tablespoon olive oil

1 teaspoon honey mustard

Salt and freshly ground black pepper

Cook the pasta according to the package directions. Drain and transfer to a large bowl. Add the giardiniera and tomatoes and stir to combine.

In a small bowl, whisk together the balsamic vinegar, oil, and honey mustard. Add the mixture to the pasta mixture and toss to coat the pasta and vegetables. Season to taste with salt and pepper.

Serve warm, at room temperature, or chilled.

Green Angel Hair with Black Olive "Eyes"

Serves 4 ■ Prep time: 15 minutes

This dish is fun and screaming with flavor from the basil pesto, olives, sun-dried tomatoes, and Parmesan cheese. When you assemble the dish, arrange the black olives so that they look like "eyes" on top of the angel hair. Sometimes I put little pieces of mozzarella cheese or sun-dried tomatoes into the center of the olives, so they look even more like eyes. For added protein, add 2 cups cubed cooked chicken.

12 ounces angel hair pasta

⅔ cup prepared basil pesto

½ cup chopped oil-packed sun-dried tomatoes

2 tablespoons grated Parmesan cheese

½ cup sliced black olives

Nutrients per serving:
Calories: 558
Fat: 25g
Saturated Fat: 4g
Cholesterol: 16mg
Carbohydrate: 70g
Protein: 18g
Fiber: 5g
Sodium: 496mg

Cook the pasta according to the package directions. Drain and transfer to a large bowl. Add the pesto and sun-dried tomatoes and stir to coat the pasta with the pesto.

Transfer the pasta to a serving platter and top with the Parmesan and olives.

Ponzu-Spiked Farfalle with Mandarin Oranges

Serves 4 ■ Prep time: 15 to 20 minutes

Ponzu sauce is a refreshing, citrus-based Asian sauce that works great in all types of dishes. In this dish, I partner the sauce with pasta, mandarin oranges, sesame oil, and cilantro. Look for ponzu sauce near the soy sauce at the grocery store. For added protein, add 2 cups cubed cooked chicken or pork or 8 ounces steamed or grilled shrimp.

The salad can be made up to 24 hours in advance and refrigerated until ready to serve. If the mixture is too thick after refrigeration, add a little more ponzu sauce to loosen it.

1 pound farfalle or bow tie pasta

1 cup ponzu sauce

1 (11-ounce) can mandarin oranges in juice, drained

2 teaspoons sesame oil

3 tablespoons chopped fresh cilantro

Salt and freshly ground black pepper

Cook the pasta according to the package directions. Drain and transfer the pasta to a large bowl. Stir in the ponzu sauce, oranges, sesame oil, and cilantro. Toss to combine. Season to taste with salt and pepper. Serve warm, at room temperature, or chilled.

Fusilli with Sun-Dried Tomatoes & Spinach

Serves 4 ■ Prep time: 15 to 20 minutes

This is a great dish for a crowd, so try it at your next party. The pasta is infused with sweet and tangy sun-dried tomatoes, herbed cheese, fresh spinach, and romano cheese. If you're not a big goat cheese fan, use Boursin or Alouette, or 4 ounces of your favorite flavored cream cheese. For added protein, add 2 cups cubed grilled or roasted chicken or steak or 8 ounces grilled or steamed shrimp. And if you like a nutty crunch, top the finished dish with ¼ cup toasted pine nuts or slivered almonds. For larger groups, simply double or triple the recipe.

Nutrients per serving:
Calories: 598
Fat: 12g
Saturated Fat: 6g
Cholesterol: 15mg
Carbohydrate: 99g
Protein: 24g
Fiber: 9g
Sodium: 354mg

1 pound fusilli

4 ounces herbed cheese (such as Boursin or Alouette)

1 cup chopped oil-packed sun-dried tomatoes

10 ounces baby spinach

Salt and freshly ground pepper

2 tablespoons grated or shredded romano cheese

Cook the pasta according to the package directions. Drain and transfer to a large bowl. While the pasta is still warm, stir in the herbed cheese, blending until the pasta is coated with the cheese. Stir in the sun-dried tomatoes and spinach (the warm pasta helps wilt the spinach). Season to taste with salt and pepper.

Transfer the pasta to a serving platter and top with the romano cheese.

Singapore Noodles with Vegetables

Serves 4 ■ Prep time: 20 to 25 minutes

Rice stick noodles are fun to cook with because they're almost translucent when they're tender. And this meal is extra easy because, with the help of frozen vegetables, you can create a colorful and complete dinner in just minutes. For added protein, add 2 cups cubed cooked chicken, pork, or steak or 8 ounces steamed or grilled shrimp. You can also add ½ cup dry-roasted cashews instead, to keep the dish vegetarian.

Nutrients per serving:
Calories: 388
Fat: 10g
Saturated Fat: 1g
Cholesterol: 0mg
Carbohydrate: 72g
Protein: 5g
Fiber: 6g
Sodium: 518mg

10 ounces rice stick noodles (rice vermicelli)
4 cups frozen mixed stir-fry vegetables (such as bell peppers and onions)
1½ cups reduced-sodium vegetable or chicken broth
½ cup mild Thai or Indian curry paste
¼ cup chopped fresh cilantro
Salt and freshly ground black pepper

Bring a large pot of water to a boil. Add the rice stick noodles and frozen vegetables and cook for 1 to 2 minutes, until the noodles are translucent and tender and the vegetables are crisp-tender. Drain and return the noodles and vegetables to the pot.

Whisk together the chicken broth and curry paste and add to the noodles and vegetables. Set the pot over medium heat and bring to a simmer. Simmer for 3 to 5 minutes, stirring frequently, until the liquid is absorbed. Remove the pan from the heat and stir in the cilantro.

Season to taste with salt and pepper. Serve warm, at room temperature, or chilled.

Wok-Seared Wontons with Baby Corn & Bok Choy

Serves 4 ■ Prep time: 15 to 20 minutes

Don't relegate your use of wonton wrappers only to pot stickers! They make an excellent addition to soups, stews, and main dishes. Think of them as "pasta squares" because they contain the same ingredients as fresh pasta (flour, water, egg). They're typically sold in the produce section of the grocery store, near the spring roll wrappers and tofu. I love adding hoisin sauce to dishes because the soy-based sauce is sweet and tangy. Look for hoisin sauce next to the soy sauce in the grocery store. When I make this dish for my family, I often add a few cloves of minced garlic (I add it when I add the ginger to the pan) and some chopped fresh cilantro (just before serving).

Nutrients per serving:
Calories: 408
Fat: 5.5g
Saturated Fat: <1g
Cholesterol: 8mg
Carbohydrate: 79g
Protein: 14g
Fiber: 6g
Sodium: 882mg

1 (12-ounce) package wonton wrappers
2 teaspoons canola oil
1 (14-ounce) can baby corn, drained
1 head bok choy, chopped
1 tablespoon minced fresh ginger
¼ cup hoisin sauce

Bring a large pot of water to a boil. Add the wonton wrappers, cook for 1 minute, and then drain.

Heat the canola oil in a large skillet or wok over medium-high heat. Add the corn, bok choy, and ginger and cook for 3 minutes, stirring frequently, until the vegetables are golden brown. Add the wontons wrappers and hoisin sauce and cook for 2 minutes to heat through, stirring constantly.

Risotto with Chicken Sausage & Caramelized Onion

Serves 4 ■ Prep time: 30 minutes

This risotto is crammed with flavor thanks to the chicken sausage and cheddar cheese. Plus, the cheese helps create a creamy, rich sauce for the short-grain Arborio rice. For variety, try the chicken sausage that contains apple; it works very well with the cheddar cheese.

The risotto can be made up to 3 days in advance and refrigerated until ready to reheat in a large saucepan. If your mixture becomes too stiff after being refrigerated, add a little broth or water when reheating to loosen it. For larger groups, simply double or triple the recipe.

Nutrients per serving:
Calories: 377
Fat: 15g
Saturated Fat: 5g
Cholesterol: 53mg
Carbohydrate: 44g
Protein: 19g
Fiber: 2g
Sodium: 479mg

2 teaspoons olive oil

½ cup chopped yellow onion

8 ounces chicken sausage, casing removed and crumbled

1 cup Arborio rice

4 to 5 cups reduced-sodium vegetable or chicken broth

½ cup shredded sharp cheddar cheese

Salt and freshly ground black pepper

Heat the oil in a large saucepan over medium heat. Add the onion and cook for 5 to 7 minutes, stirring frequently, until the onion is golden brown and caramelized. Add the sausage and cook for 3 minutes, or until browned, breaking up the sausage as it cooks. Add the rice and cook for 3 minutes, stirring frequently, until the rice becomes translucent. Add ½ cup of the broth and stir until the broth is absorbed. Add another ½ cup of the broth and cook until the liquid is absorbed. Continue adding the broth, ½ cup at a time (add the next ½ cup once the liquid from the previous ½ cup is absorbed), for 15 to 20 minutes, until the rice is tender and the mixture is creamy, stirring frequently.

Add the cheddar cheese and cook until the cheese melts, adding more broth if necessary and stirring constantly. Season to taste with salt and pepper.

Summer Corn Risotto with Parmesan

Serves 4 ■ Prep time: 30 minutes

I call this "summer" corn risotto, but you can make it year-round thanks to frozen corn. The sweetness of the corn coupled with the sharpness of the Parmesan cheese is divine. For super-finicky eaters, leave out the garlic.

The risotto can be made up to 3 days in advance and refrigerated until ready to reheat in a large saucepan. If your mixture becomes stiff after being refrigerated, add a little broth or water when reheating to loosen it. For larger groups, simply double or triple the recipe.

Nutrients per serving:
Calories: 406
Fat: 7g
Saturated Fat: 2g
Cholesterol: 4mg
Carbohydrate: 78g
Protein: 16g
Fiber: 6g
Sodium: 155mg

Cooking spray
4 cups thawed frozen white corn or yellow and white corn blend
Salt and freshly ground black pepper
2 teaspoons olive oil
1 cup Arborio rice
2 cloves garlic, minced
4 to 5 cups reduced-sodium vegetable or chicken broth
¼ cup grated Parmesan cheese

Preheat the oven to 400°F. Coat a large baking sheet with cooking spray.

Spread the corn out on the prepared baking sheet and season to taste with salt and pepper. Roast the corn for 10 to 15 minutes, stirring halfway through cooking, until golden brown.

Heat the oil in a large saucepan over medium heat. Add the rice and garlic and cook for 3 minutes, stirring frequently, until the rice becomes translucent. Add ½ cup of the broth and stir until the broth is absorbed. Add another ½ cup of the broth and cook until the liquid is absorbed. Continue adding the broth, ½ cup at a time (add the next ½ cup once the liquid from the previous ½ cup is absorbed), for 15 to 20 minutes, until the rice is tender and the mixture is creamy, stirring frequently.

Add the Parmesan and cook until the cheese melts, adding more broth if necessary and stirring constantly. Season to taste with salt and pepper.

Herbed Ricotta–Stuffed Shells

Serves 4 ■ Prep time: 20 minutes ■ Cooking time: 45 minutes

This is a great dish for those of you who like to preplan, because it's an ideal make-ahead meal for family and friends. I infuse ricotta cheese with herbed soft cheese before stuffing the creamy mixture into the tender shells. If you want vegetables in the filling, add 1 cup sautéed sliced mushrooms or 1 cup frozen chopped spinach that's been thawed and well drained. To reduce the amount of sodium in the dish, select a reduced-sodium brand of pasta sauce.

The shells can be made up to 3 days in advance and refrigerated until ready to bake. You can also freeze the assembled shells for up to 3 months. Thaw completely in the refrigerator before baking. For larger groups, simply double or triple the recipe.

Nutrients per serving:
Calories: 610
Fat: 20g
Saturated Fat: 11g
Cholesterol: 56mg
Carbohydrate: 81g
Protein: 30g
Fiber: 5g
Sodium: 816mg

12 ounces large pasta shells

1½ cups part-skim ricotta cheese

4 ounces herbed cheese (such as Boursin or Alouette)

1½ cups pasta sauce of your choice

2 tablespoons grated Parmesan cheese

Preheat the oven to 350°F.

Cook the pasta shells according to the package instructions, and then drain.

Meanwhile, in a large bowl, combine the ricotta and herbed cheese. Mix well. Spoon the mixture into the cooked shells.

Spoon ½ cup of the pasta sauce into the bottom of a shallow baking dish that will just fit the shells in a single layer. Arrange the stuffed shells on top of the sauce. Spoon the remaining sauce over the shells and top with the Parmesan. Cover the dish with aluminum foil and bake for 30 minutes. Uncover and bake for 15 more minutes, until the top is golden brown.

Grilled Chicken Strips with Orange Marmalade Ketchup

Serves 4 ■ Prep time: 10 minutes ■ Cooking time: 5 minutes

Infusing smoky ketchup with orange marmalade creates a perfect balance of flavors that all family members will love. It's sweet, salty, and smoky, and excellent with grilled chicken. For birthday parties, serve the chicken strips on a big platter with the Sweet Potato Fries with Maple-Dijon Dip (page 187). For larger groups, simply double or triple the recipe.

Cooking spray
1 pound boneless, skinless chicken breasts, cut into 1-inch-thick strips
Salt and freshly ground black pepper
½ cup ketchup
½ cup orange marmalade
1 teaspoon Dijon mustard
1 teaspoon liquid smoke

Nutrients per serving:
Calories: 269
Fat: 3g
Saturated Fat: 1g
Cholesterol: 72mg
Carbohydrate: 34g
Protein: 27g
Fiber: 1g
Sodium: 450mg

Coat a stovetop grill pan or griddle with cooking spray and preheat over medium-high heat. Season the chicken strips with salt and pepper. Add the chicken strips to the hot pan and cook for 3 to 5 minutes, turning frequently, until golden brown and cooked through.

Meanwhile, in a small saucepan, combine the ketchup, marmalade, mustard, and liquid smoke. Mix well and set the pan over medium heat. Bring to a simmer, then decrease the heat to low and simmer for 5 minutes.

Serve the chicken strips with the warm ketchup mixture on the side for dunking.

Chicken-Fried Chicken with Country-Style Buttermilk-Bacon Sauce

Serves 4 ■ Prep time: 10 minutes ■ Cooking time: 10 minutes

Nutrients per serving:
Calories: 256
Fat: 11g
Saturated Fat: 4g
Cholesterol: 88mg
Carbohydrate: 5g
Protein: 34g
Fiber: 0g
Sodium: 320mg

The secret to creating perfectly coated chicken is double-dipping the chicken breasts in the ranch dip (with a quick egg white layer in between). The double layers create a fabulous crust that also helps thicken the sauce to make gravy.

The chicken can be prepped (coated with the ranch coating) up to 24 hours in advance and refrigerated until ready to bake.

> **4 boneless, skinless chicken breast halves (about 4 ounces each)**
> **Salt and freshly ground black pepper**
> **1 (1-ounce) packet powdered buttermilk ranch dip**
> **2 large egg whites**
> **1 tablespoon olive oil**
> **1½ cups low-fat (1%) milk**
> **4 slices center-cut bacon, cooked until crisp and crumbled**

Pound the chicken between two pieces of plastic wrap until ½ inch thick. Season both sides of the chicken with salt and pepper. Place the ranch dip in a shallow dish. Place the egg whites in another shallow dish.

Add the chicken to the ranch dip and turn to coat both sides. Transfer the chicken to the egg whites and turn to coat both sides. Return the chicken to the ranch dip and turn to coat both sides.

Heat the oil in a large skillet over medium-high heat. Add the chicken and cook for 2 minutes per side, or until golden brown. Add the milk and bacon and bring to a simmer. Simmer for 3 to 5 minutes, until the chicken is cooked through and the sauce thickens.

Grilled Chicken with Cantaloupe, Cucumber & Lime Salsa

Serves 4 ■ Prep time: 10 minutes ■ Cooking time: 10 minutes

The sweetness of the cantaloupe partners perfectly with the tart lime and herbal cilantro. I also like spooning this salsa over grilled or roasted fish or pork. Or just serve it with a basket of baked tortilla chips. If you'd rather roast the chicken, place the chicken breasts on a baking sheet and roast at 400°F for 25 minutes.

The salsa can be prepared up to 24 hours in advance and refrigerated until ready to serve.

Nutrients per serving:
Calories: 159
Fat: 3g
Saturated Fat: 1g
Cholesterol: 72mg
Carbohydrate: 4g
Protein: 27g
Fiber: 1g
Sodium: 70mg

Cooking spray
4 boneless, skinless chicken breast halves (about 4 ounces each)
Salt and freshly ground black pepper
1 cup diced cantaloupe
1 cup diced English (seedless) cucumber
Juice and zest of 1 lime
2 tablespoons chopped fresh cilantro

Coat a stovetop grill pan or griddle with cooking spray and preheat over medium-high heat. Season both sides of the chicken with salt and pepper. Place the chicken on the hot pan and cook for 3 to 5 minutes per side, until the chicken is golden brown and cooked through.

Meanwhile, in a medium bowl, combine the cantaloupe, cucumber, 1 tablespoon of the lime juice, 1 teaspoon of the lime zest, and the cilantro. Season the salsa with salt and pepper.

Arrange the chicken on a serving platter and spoon the salsa over the top.

Chicken Pot Pie with Peas & Carrots

Serves 4 ■ Prep time: 10 minutes ■ Cooking time: 20 to 25 minutes
Cooling time: 10 minutes

Nutrients per serving:
Calories: 627
Fat: 37g
Saturated Fat: 10g
Cholesterol: 98mg
Carbohydrate: 36g
Protein: 36g
Fiber: 3g
Sodium: 441mg

Few things are more comforting than pot pies. What's not comforting is the labor often required to make them. My version is different—you don't need loads of ingredients because I get full flavor from cremini mushrooms, herbed cheese, and a flaky and elegant puff pastry top. This meal is also finicky friendly because you can add your family's favorite vegetables and mix and match the filling to suit your needs.

The pot pie can be assembled up to 24 hours in advance and refrigerated until ready to bake.

2 teaspoons olive oil
1 pound boneless, skinless chicken breasts, cut into 1-inch pieces
8 ounces cremini mushrooms, sliced
4 ounces herbed cheese (such as Boursin or Alouette)
1 cup frozen peas and carrots
1 sheet frozen puff pastry, thawed according to package directions
Cooking spray

Preheat the oven to 400°F.

Heat the oil in a large skillet over medium-high heat. Add the chicken and cook for 3 minutes, stirring frequently, until golden brown on all sides. Add the mushrooms and cook for 3 minutes, or until the mushrooms are tender and releasing liquid. Stir in the herbed cheese and the frozen peas and carrots and mix well.

Transfer the mixture to a shallow baking dish (about 11 by 7 inches).

Unroll the pastry and roll the sheet into an 11 by 7-inch rectangle (or the size of your baking dish). Place the pastry over the chicken mixture and press the pastry to the rim of the dish to seal. Spray the surface of the pastry with cooking spray. Using a sharp knife, cut several slits in the pastry.

Bake for 20 to 25 minutes, until the pastry is golden brown and the filling is hot and bubbly. Let cool for 10 minutes before serving.

Chicken & Chile Cream Cheese Wraps

Serves 4 ■ Prep time: 10 minutes

Nutrients per serving:

Calories: 328

Fat: 13g

Saturated Fat: 7g

Cholesterol: 86mg

Carbohydrate: 21g

Protein: 30g

Fiber: 2g

Sodium: 634mg

Canned green chile peppers are available in mild, medium, and hot versions. They add great color and a wonderful roasted chile flavor to a variety of dishes. Look for them next to the other Mexican ingredients in the grocery store. For added flavor, add chopped fresh cilantro to the wraps. You can also add vegetables—I like to add prepackaged broccoli slaw, red lettuce, or baby spinach for color and crunch. For finicky eaters, select mild green chiles or eliminate the chiles and use vegetable cream cheese instead of regular.

The wraps can be assembled up to 24 hours in advance and refrigerated until ready to serve. For larger groups, simply double or triple the recipe.

8 ounces light cream cheese, softened

1 (4-ounce) can diced green chiles

1 teaspoon chili powder

4 fajita-size flour tortillas (regular or whole wheat)

2 cups shredded cooked chicken breast (poached, grilled, roasted, or rotisserie)

In a medium bowl, combine the cream cheese, chiles, and chili powder. Mix well. Spread the mixture onto the tortillas, to within ¼ inch of the edges. Top the cream cheese mixture with the chicken. Roll up tightly.

Orange Chicken with Bok Choy

Serves 4 ■ Prep time: 10 minutes ■ Cooking time: 10 minutes

The sweet orange marmalade pairs perfectly with the salty soy sauce in this chicken dish. If desired, you can substitute apricot preserves or any seedless preserves or jam for the marmalade. I like to serve the chicken and bok choy mixture over rice or rice noodles and, for added flavor and color, I sometimes add chopped fresh cilantro just before serving.

1 tablespoon canola oil

1 pound boneless, skinless chicken breasts, cut into 1-inch pieces

1 large head bok choy, chopped

1 cup orange marmalade

2 tablespoons reduced-sodium soy sauce

2 teaspoons toasted sesame oil

Salt and freshly ground black pepper

Heat the canola oil in a large skillet over medium-high heat. Add the chicken and cook for 3 to 5 minutes, stirring frequently, until golden brown on all sides. Add the bok choy and cook for 2 minutes, or until the green leaves begin to soften. Add the marmalade, soy sauce, and sesame oil and bring to a simmer. Simmer for 2 to 3 minutes, until the chicken is cooked through. Season to taste with salt and pepper.

Nutrients per serving:

Calories: 420

Fat: 9g

Saturated Fat: 1.5g

Cholesterol: 72mg

Carbohydrate: 58g

Protein: 30g

Fiber: 3g

Sodium: 544mg

Parmesan & Pecan–Crusted Chicken

Serves 4 ■ Prep time: 10 minutes ■ Cooking time: 20 to 25 minutes

Thanks to the use of egg whites, the coating on this chicken is light, nutty, and crunchy due to the chopped pecans and Parmesan cheese. For birthday parties, cut the chicken into strips (fingers) and decrease the cooking time to 15 minutes. When serving folks who don't like pecans, you may substitute walnuts, almonds, or pine nuts.

Leftovers will keep for up to 3 days in the refrigerator, so make extra for later in the week. For larger groups, simply double or triple the recipe.

Nutrients per serving:
Calories: 371
Fat: 24g
Saturated Fat: 3g
Cholesterol: 77mg
Carbohydrate: 7g
Protein: 33g
Fiber: 3g
Sodium: 167mg

Cooking spray
1 cup whole pecans
¼ cup grated Parmesan cheese
2 tablespoons all-purpose flour
2 egg whites
4 boneless, skinless chicken breast halves (about 4 ounces each)
Salt and freshly ground black pepper

Preheat the oven to 375°F. Coat a large baking sheet with cooking spray.

In a food processor, combine the pecans and Parmesan and process until finely ground. Transfer the mixture to a shallow dish. Place the flour in another shallow dish, and place the egg whites in a third shallow dish.

Season both sides of the chicken with salt and pepper. Add the chicken to the flour, and turn to coat both sides. Transfer the chicken to the egg whites, and turn to coat both sides. Transfer the chicken to the pecan-Parmesan mixture, and turn to coat both sides.

Place the chicken on the prepared baking sheet and spray the surface of the chicken with cooking spray.

Bake for 20 to 25 minutes, until the chicken is golden brown and cooked through.

Grilled Chicken with Balsamic Syrup & Crumbled Feta

Serves 4 ■ Prep time: 10 minutes ■ Cooking time: 15 to 20 minutes

I adore reducing balsamic vinegar down to a thick syrup. You can drizzle the sweet and tangy glaze over practically anything—chicken, beef, pork, fish, and vegetables. It adds a wonderful, almost complex liveliness, and it's just one ingredient. In this dish, I drizzle the syrup over chicken and then add salty feta cheese and sweet green chives. You can make the balsamic reduction in advance and refrigerate it until ready to use (it will last at least one week). If the syrup becomes too firm to pour, add a little water and warm the syrup in a small saucepan over low heat until you reach the desired consistency.

Nutrients per serving:
Calories: 289
Fat: 5g
Saturated Fat: 2.3g
Cholesterol: 81mg
Carbohydrate: 27g
Protein: 28g
Fiber: <1g
Sodium: 193mg

1½ cups balsamic vinegar

3 tablespoons light brown sugar

Cooking spray

4 boneless skinless chicken breast halves (about 4 ounces each)

Salt and freshly ground black pepper

¼ cup crumbled feta cheese

2 tablespoons chopped fresh chives

In a small saucepan, whisk together the vinegar and sugar and set the pan over medium heat. Bring to a simmer. Reduce the heat to low and simmer for 15 to 20 minutes, until the mixture reduces to ½ cup, stirring frequently.

Meanwhile, coat a stove-top grill pan or griddle with cooking spray and preheat over medium-high heat. Season both sides of the chicken with the salt and pepper. Add the chicken to the hot pan and cook for 3 to 5 minutes per side, until cooked through. Transfer the chicken to a serving plate. Drizzle the balsamic syrup over the chicken and top with the feta and chives.

Chicken Pops with Creamy Barbecue Dip

Serves 4 ■ Prep time: 10 to 15 minutes ■ Cooking time: 5 minutes

In this dish, I add a little sour cream to the prepared barbecue sauce to create a creamy blend the whole family will adore. You can add any additional ingredients to the skewers that you like: Button mushrooms, zucchini, yellow summer squash, and red onion all make great choices. To make sure the dish is gluten-free, read the label on the barbecue sauce.

When using wooden skewers, soak them in water for at least 10 minutes before using to prevent them from burning. You will need 8 to 10 skewers. For larger groups, simply double or triple the recipe.

Nutrients per serving:
Calories: 188
Fat: 4g
Saturated Fat: 1g
Cholesterol: 74mg
Carbohydrate: 10g
Protein: 27g
Fiber: 1g
Sodium: 265mg

Cooking spray

1 pound boneless, skinless chicken breasts, cut into 2-inch pieces

1½ cups cherry or grape tomatoes

1 large green bell pepper, seeded and cut into 2-inch pieces

Salt and freshly ground black pepper

¼ cup barbecue sauce of your choice

1 tablespoon light sour cream

Coat a stovetop grill pan or griddle with cooking spray and preheat over medium-high heat.

Skewer the chicken pieces, tomatoes, and bell pepper pieces on metal or wooden skewers. Season the chicken and vegetables with salt and pepper.

In a small bowl, whisk together the barbecue sauce and sour cream. Brush the mixture all over the chicken and vegetables.

Add the skewers to the hot pan and cook for 5 minutes, turning frequently, until the chicken is cooked through and the vegetables are crisp-tender.

Chicken Fingers with Peanut Sauce

Serves 4 ■ Prep time: 10 minutes ■ Cooking time: 20 minutes

Kids love to dunk chicken fingers into dipping sauce. This one is sweet from the peanut butter and coconut milk and a little salty from the soy sauce—an excellent balance of flavors. You can also serve the peanut sauce with grilled or steamed shrimp or grilled tofu.

The coconut-peanut sauce can be made up to 3 days in advance and refrigerated until ready to reheat in a saucepan or in the microwave. That said, I advise you to make an extra batch for future meals (or extra dipping!). For larger groups, simply double or triple the recipe.

Nutrients per serving:
Calories: 434
Fat: 32g
Saturated Fat: 21g
Cholesterol: 72mg
Carbohydrate: 7g
Protein: 33g
Fiber: 2g
Sodium: 449mg

Cooking spray
1 pound boneless, skinless chicken breasts, cut into thin strips
Salt and freshly ground black pepper
1 (14-ounce) can coconut milk
¼ cup creamy peanut butter
2 tablespoons reduced-sodium soy sauce

Preheat the oven to 400°F. Coat a large baking sheet with cooking spray.

Season the chicken strips with salt and pepper and arrange on the prepared baking sheet. Bake for 20 minutes, or until the chicken is golden brown and cooked through.

Meanwhile, in a small saucepan, whisk together the coconut milk, peanut butter, and soy sauce. Set the pan over medium-low heat and bring to a gentle simmer, stirring constantly. Simmer for 3 to 5 minutes.

Serve the chicken fingers with the peanut sauce on the side for dunking.

Baked Chicken with Pears & Red Onion

Serves 4 ■ Prep time: 10 to 15 minutes ■ Cooking time: 25 minutes

The topping on this chicken showcases a marvelous blend of flavors: sweet pears with salty feta cheese. To please finicky eaters, you may replace the onion with apples and eliminate the feta cheese (or just add the feta to the adult portions).

Nutrients per serving:
Calories: 250
Fat: 7g
Saturated Fat: 4g
Cholesterol: 89mg
Carbohydrate: 17g
Protein: 30g
Fiber: 3g
Sodium: 274mg

Cooking spray

4 boneless, skinless chicken breast halves (about 4 ounces each)

Salt and freshly ground black pepper

2 ripe pears, cored and diced (peeled if desired)

½ cup diced red onion

1 teaspoon dried oregano

½ cup crumbled feta cheese

Preheat the oven to 375°F. Coat a shallow baking dish with cooking spray.

Season both sides of the chicken with salt and pepper. Arrange the chicken in the bottom of the prepared dish.

In a medium bowl, toss together the pears, onion, and oregano. Spoon the mixture over the chicken in the baking dish. Cover the dish with aluminum foil and bake for 15 minutes.

Uncover the chicken, sprinkle the feta cheese over the top, and bake for 10 more minutes, or until the chicken is cooked through.

Chicken Fingers with Almond "Nails"

Serves 4 ■ Prep time: 10 minutes ■ Cooking time: 20 minutes

This is the perfect dinner treat for Halloween because, thanks to sliced almonds, the chicken strips really look like fingers! The honey mustard not only helps the almonds stick to the chicken but also adds terrific flavor. Partner the chicken with Green Angel Hair with Black Olive "Eyes" (page 81) and White Chocolate–Dipped Strawberry Screamers (page 204). If desired, serve the chicken fingers with additional honey mustard or barbecue sauce on the side for dunking. For larger groups, simply double or triple the recipe.

Nutrients per serving:
Calories: 182
Fat: 6g
Saturated Fat: 1g
Cholesterol: 72mg
Carbohydrate: 3g
Protein: 28g
Fiber: 1g
Sodium: 95mg

Cooking spray
1 pound boneless, skinless chicken breasts, cut into thin strips
Salt and freshly ground black pepper
1 tablespoon honey mustard
¼ cup sliced blanched almonds

Preheat the oven to 400°F. Coat a large baking sheet with cooking spray.

Season the chicken strips with salt and pepper and arrange on the prepared baking sheet.

Brush the honey mustard all over the top of each chicken strip. Arrange a sliced almond on the end of each chicken finger, making a "fingernail."

Bake the chicken for 20 minutes, or until cooked through and golden brown.

Chicken Enchiladas with Pepper Jack & Sour Cream

Serves 8 ■ Prep time: 10 to 15 minutes ■ Cooking time: 20 minutes

Enchiladas may look hard to make, but they're actually quite simple. This tortilla filling is loaded with chicken, sour cream, and pepper Jack cheese, and the topping of salsa keeps everything moist and flavorful as the casserole bakes in the oven. For finicky eaters, pick a salsa variety you know the whole family will enjoy and substitute Monterey Jack cheese for the pepper Jack, if desired.

The enchiladas can be assembled up to 24 hours in advance and refrigerated until ready to bake.

Nutrients per serving:
Calories: 377
Fat: 17g
Saturated Fat: 8g
Cholesterol: 100mg
Carbohydrate: 21g
Protein: 33g
Fiber: 1g
Sodium: 569mg

Cooking spray
4 cups shredded cooked chicken (poached, grilled, roasted, or rotisserie)
1 cup light sour cream
2 cups shredded pepper Jack cheese
8 fajita-size flour tortillas (regular or whole wheat)
1 cup salsa of your choice

Preheat the oven to 375°F. Coat a shallow baking dish with cooking spray.

In a large bowl, combine the chicken, sour cream, and 1 cup of the cheese, mixing well.

Arrange the tortillas on a flat surface. Spoon the chicken mixture onto the center of each tortilla. Roll up the tortillas and place in the bottom of the prepared pan, seam side down. Spoon the salsa over the tortillas and top with the remaining 1 cup cheese.

Bake for 20 minutes, or until the cheese is bubbly.

Individual Chicken & Cheese Calzones

Serves 4 ■ Prep time: 15 minutes ■ Cooking time: 15 to 20 minutes

Individual calzones are not only fun to make and eat, but they're also true crowd-pleasers because each one can be customized. This version has mozzarella cheese and chicken, but you can add practically anything you want. I always add vegetables to filling—our favorites are broccoli florets and chopped spinach (when using frozen spinach, thaw and drain it very well and pat it dry before adding to the filling). To reduce the amount of sodium, opt for reduced-sodium pasta sauce.

The calzones can be assembled up to 24 hours in advance and refrigerated until ready to bake. You can also freeze the assembled calzones for up to 3 months. Thaw completely in the refrigerator before baking. For larger groups, simply double or triple the recipe.

Nutrients per serving:
Calories: 588
Fat: 21g
Saturated Fat: 9g
Cholesterol: 95mg
Carbohydrate: 55g
Protein: 48g
Fiber: 3g
Sodium: 925mg

Cooking spray
1 pound frozen bread dough, thawed according to package directions
2 cups shredded part-skim mozzarella cheese
2 cups shredded or cubed cooked chicken breast (poached, grilled, roasted, or rotisserie)
2 teaspoons salt-free Italian seasoning
1 cup marinara or pizza sauce of your choice

Preheat the oven to 400°F. Coat a large baking sheet with cooking spray.

Divide the dough into 4 equal pieces. Roll each piece out into a circle about ½ inch thick and 6 to 8 inches in diameter.

In a medium bowl, combine the cheese, chicken, and Italian seasoning. Spoon the mixture onto one half of each dough circle, to within ½ inch of the edges. Pull the untopped side of dough up and over the filling and pinch the edges together to seal into a half-moon shape. Transfer the calzones to the prepared baking sheet and spray the surface of the calzones with cooking spray.

Bake for 15 to 20 minutes, until the calzones are puffed up and golden brown. Meanwhile, warm the marinara sauce in a saucepan. Serve the calzones with the warm sauce on the side for dunking.

Chicken Burgers with Soy-Cilantro Glaze

Serves 4 ■ Prep time: 10 minutes ■ Cooking time: 10 minutes

I like to serve these moist, scallion-spiked burgers over shredded lettuce or alongside Asian noodles—the soy-honey glaze partners well with other Asian ingredients. You can also serve the burgers on hamburger buns or inside pita pockets. For finicky eaters, eliminate the scallions from the burgers and the cilantro from the glaze.

You can make a big batch of the burgers and freeze them for up to 3 months before cooking. Thaw the burgers completely in the refrigerator before cooking.

Nutrients per serving:
Calories: 208
Fat: 9g
Saturated Fat: 3g
Cholesterol: 91mg
Carbohydrate: 11g
Protein: 21g
Fiber: <1g
Sodium: 580mg

Cooking spray
1 pound ground chicken
¼ cup chopped scallions (white and green parts)
Salt and freshly ground black pepper
⅓ cup reduced-sodium soy sauce
2 tablespoons honey
2 tablespoons chopped fresh cilantro

Coat a stovetop grill pan or griddle with cooking spray and preheat over medium-high heat.

In a large bowl, combine the chicken and scallions. Season with about ¼ teaspoon salt and ¼ teaspoon pepper and mix well to combine. Shape the mixture into 4 equal patties about 1 inch thick. Add the burgers to the hot pan and cook for 3 to 5 minutes per side, until cooked through.

Meanwhile, in a small saucepan, combine the soy sauce and honey. Set the pan over medium heat and bring to a simmer. Simmer until the mixture thickens and reduces to about ¼ cup. Remove the glaze from the heat and stir in the cilantro. Drizzle the glaze over the burgers.

Shredded Barbecue Chicken with Apple Slaw

Serves 4 ■ Prep time: 10 minutes ■ Cooking time: 5 minutes

I like to serve this chicken piled high on the slaw, but you can also turn this into a sandwich and serve the chicken and slaw on hamburger buns, French rolls, or ciabatta rolls. The sweetness of the apples makes the slaw super finicky friendly, so choose your family's favorite apple variety (just make sure it's got a nice sweetness and isn't too tart). And because I adore blue cheese with apples and barbecue chicken, I use a good-quality dressing. For finicky eaters who don't like blue cheese, substitute light coleslaw dressing, ranch dressing, or mayonnaise.

The chicken mixture and slaw are so wonderful that you'll want to make big batches of both and store them separately in the refrigerator (both will keep for up to 3 days). For larger groups, simply double or triple the recipe.

Nutrients per serving:
Calories: 546
Fat: 8g
Saturated Fat: 2g
Cholesterol: 119mg
Carbohydrate: 71g
Protein: 47g
Fiber: 6g
Sodium: 671mg

> **4 cups shredded cooked chicken breast (poached, grilled, roasted, or rotisserie)**
> **2 cups low-sodium barbecue sauce of your choice**
> **1 (16-ounce) package coleslaw mix**
> **2 McIntosh, Gala, or Fuji apples, cored and shredded**
> **½ cup light blue cheese salad dressing, plus more if desired**

Combine the chicken and barbecue sauce in a medium saucepan over medium heat. Bring to a simmer. Simmer for 3 minutes, stirring frequently, until the chicken is heated through.

Meanwhile, in a large bowl, combine the slaw mix, apples, and dressing. Mix well to combine. Spoon the apple slaw onto individual plates and top with the chicken mixture.

Apricot & Lime–Glazed Chicken

Serves 4 ■ Prep time: 5 minutes ■ Cooking time: 10 minutes

This finicky friendly dish balances the flavors of sweet apricot preserves with tart lime and salty teriyaki sauce. You may use orange marmalade instead of apricot preserves, if you prefer. I often serve the chicken and sauce over rice, couscous, or quinoa to make sure every drop of the delicious sauce is absorbed.

Nutrients per serving:
Calories: 370
Fat: 7g
Saturated Fat: 1g
Cholesterol: 72mg
Carbohydrate: 53g
Protein: 27g
Fiber: <1g
Sodium: 174mg

1 tablespoon canola oil
4 boneless, skinless chicken breast halves (about 4 ounces each)
Salt and freshly ground black pepper
1 cup apricot preserves
Juice and zest of 1 lime
1 tablespoon reduced-sodium teriyaki sauce

Heat the oil in a large skillet over medium-high heat. Season both sides of the chicken with salt and pepper. Add the chicken to the hot pan and cook for 2 minutes per side, until golden brown. Add the preserves, 1 tablespoon of the lime juice, 1 teaspoon of the lime zest, and the teriyaki sauce and bring to a simmer. Decrease the heat to medium and simmer for 5 minutes, or until the chicken is cooked through.

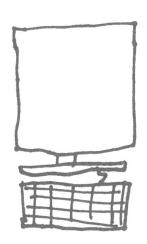

Chicken Mozzarella with Buttered Spaghetti

Serves 4 ■ Prep time: 10 minutes ■ Cooking time: 25 to 30 minutes

I call this chicken mozzarella instead of chicken Parmesan because I use only mozzarella cheese instead of the usual combination of cheeses. You can sprinkle grated Parmesan cheese over the mozzarella before baking the chicken, if desired. For a meatless version, make this dish with 8 stemmed portobello mushroom caps instead of the chicken breasts. For added flavor in the spaghetti, add 2 tablespoons grated Parmesan cheese when you add the butter. You may also stir in 1/4 cup chopped fresh basil.

The chicken can be assembled up to 24 hours in advance and refrigerated until ready to bake. For larger groups, simply double or triple the recipe.

Nutrients per serving:

Calories: 517

Fat: 16g

Saturated Fat: 8g

Cholesterol: 103mg

Carbohydrate: 48g

Protein: 42g

Fiber: 3g

Sodium: 363mg

Cooking spray

4 boneless, skinless chicken breast halves (about 4 ounces each)

Salt and freshly ground black pepper

1 cup pasta sauce of your choice

1 cup shredded part-skim mozzarella cheese

8 ounces spaghetti

2 tablespoons unsalted butter

Preheat the oven to 375°F. Coat a shallow baking dish with cooking spray.

Place the chicken between two pieces of plastic wrap and pound until 1 inch thick (use the flat side of a meat mallet or a heavy rolling pin). Arrange the chicken in the prepared dish and season with salt and pepper. Spoon the sauce over the chicken and top with the cheese.

Bake for 25 to 30 minutes, until the chicken is cooked through and the cheese is bubbly.

Meanwhile, cook the spaghetti according to the package directions. Drain and transfer to a large bowl. While still warm, add the butter to the spaghetti and stir to coat. Season to taste with salt and pepper.

Serve the chicken with the spaghetti on the side.

Chicken Sausage & Sweet Onion Pizza

Serves 4 ■ Prep time: 20 minutes ■ Cooking time: 15 to 20 minutes

I like the pairing of chicken sausage with the cheese, onion, and oregano on this pizza, but you could use turkey sausage (sweet or hot) instead. I also like the nuttiness of fontina, but feel free to try provolone, Gruyère, or Gouda. For larger groups, simply double or triple the recipe and make multiple pizzas.

Nutrients per serving:
Calories: 387
Fat: 18g
Saturated Fat: 5g
Cholesterol: 54mg
Carbohydrate: 45g
Protein: 17g
Fiber: 2g
Sodium: 756mg

1 tablespoon olive oil
1 cup thinly sliced yellow onion
1 (14-ounce) can refrigerated pizza dough
8 ounces chicken sausage, casing removed
½ cup shredded fontina cheese
½ teaspoon dried oregano

Preheat the oven to 400°F.

Heat the oil in a large skillet over medium heat. Add the onion and cook for 5 to 7 minutes, stirring frequently, until golden brown.

Unroll the dough onto a baking sheet and press out into a 12 by 8-inch rectangle. Arrange the onion all over the dough, to within ¼ inch of the edges. Set aside.

Place the sausage in the same skillet that you used for the onion and set the pan over medium-high heat. Cook for 5 to 7 minutes, until the sausage is cooked through, breaking up the meat as it cooks. Arrange the sausage on top of the onion. Top with the cheese and oregano.

Bake for 15 to 20 minutes, until the crust is golden brown and the cheese is bubbly.

Sun-Dried Tomato Cups with Mexican Chicken

Serves 4 ■ Prep time: 10 minutes ■ Cooking time: 6 to 8 minutes

Nutrients per serving:
Calories: 519
Fat: 13g
Saturated Fat: 3.7g
Cholesterol: 123mg
Carbohydrate: 46g
Protein: 49g
Fiber: 3g
Sodium: 986mg

This dish is a unique, colorful, and fun way to season and serve plain-old chicken. In fact, it's an excellent way to utilize leftovers, and any cooked chicken will work (baked, broiled, roasted, rotisserie). The "cups" are made by pressing flour tortillas into muffin cups and then baking them until crisp. Think of this recipe as a flour tortilla–version of taco salad. I use flavored flour tortillas, but feel free to use any tortilla flavor and variety you want, including garden spinach and multi-grain. You can also add a variety of toppings, such as sliced black olives, pickled jalapeno peppers (unless you have a finicky eater that doesn't like heat!), and shredded cheddar cheese. Also, the tortilla cups can be made up to 24 hours in advance and stored at room temperature until ready to fill.

- **4 large (10-inch) sun-dried tomato flour tortillas, halved**
- **4 cups diced or shredded cooked chicken breast (poached, grilled, roasted, or rotisserie)**
- **1 cup salsa of your choice**
- **½ cup frozen yellow or white corn, thawed**
- **¼ cup light ranch dressing**
- **Salt and freshly ground black pepper to taste**

Preheat the oven to 400°F.

Using two hands, bring the two ends of the tortillas together to form a cone shape. Press the cone-shaped tortillas into the bottom and up the sides of 8 cups of a 12-cup muffin tin. Bake for 6 to 8 minutes, until the tortillas are crisp.

Meanwhile, in a medium bowl, combine the chicken, salsa, corn, and ranch dressing. Mix well. Season to taste with salt and pepper.

Spoon the chicken mixture into the tortilla cups and serve.

Molasses, Balsamic & Mustard Turkey Tenderloin

Serves 4 ■ Prep time: 5 minutes ■ Cooking time: 25 minutes
Standing time: 10 minutes

Nutrients per serving:
Calories: 203
Fat: 1g
Saturated Fat: 0g
Cholesterol: 34mg
Carbohydrate: 28g
Protein: 22g
Fiber: 1g
Sodium: 150mg

The recipe title says it all: sweet molasses, tangy vinegar, and spicy mustard make a glaze for moist turkey tenderloin. Baby carrots are the ideal accompaniment because they add a nice sweetness and burst of color. To round out the meal without using another pan, arrange cubed Yukon gold or red potatoes among the carrots in the baking dish.

The turkey can be assembled (with the carrots and glaze) up to 24 hours ahead of time and refrigerated until ready to bake.

Cooking spray
1 (1-pound) turkey tenderloin
Salt and freshly ground black pepper
2 cups baby carrots
⅓ cup molasses
2 tablespoons balsamic vinegar
2 teaspoons Dijon mustard

Preheat the oven to 400°F. Coat a shallow baking dish with cooking spray.

Season the turkey tenderloin with salt and pepper and place in the prepared baking dish. Arrange the baby carrots around the turkey in the pan.

In a small bowl, whisk together the molasses, vinegar, and mustard. Pour the mixture all over the turkey tenderloin.

Bake for 25 minutes, or until an instant-read thermometer inserted in the center reads 160°F. Let the turkey tenderloin stand for 10 minutes before slicing crosswise into ½-inch-thick rounds.

Turkey Meatball Sliders

Serves 4 ■ Prep time: 10 minutes ■ Cooking time: 10 minutes

I often nestle these heavenly turkey meatballs on Hawaiian rolls because the sweetness of the rolls complements the savory meatballs. Be sure to select your family's favorite pasta or pizza sauce for simmering the meatballs and, if desired, drape a slice of mozzarella or provolone cheese over the meatballs once they're on the rolls. For added flavor in the meatballs, add 2 teaspoons salt-free Italian seasoning or 1 teaspoon dried oregano.

The meatballs can be made up to 3 days in advance and refrigerated until ready to reheat in a large saucepan. You can also freeze the cooked meatballs in the sauce for up to 3 months. Thaw completely in the refrigerator before reheating in a saucepan. For larger groups, simply double or triple the recipe.

Nutrients per serving:
Calories: 439
Fat: 14g
Saturated Fat: 3g
Cholesterol: 86mg
Carbohydrate: 46g
Protein: 34g
Fiber: 3g
Sodium: 765mg

1 pound ground turkey
¼ cup grated Parmesan cheese
1 large egg, lightly beaten
Salt and freshly ground black pepper
1 tablespoon olive oil
1½ cups pasta or pizza sauce of your choice
12 small soft dinner rolls, split

In a large bowl, combine the ground turkey, Parmesan, egg, about ¼ teaspoon salt, and about ¼ teaspoon pepper. Mix well and shape the mixture into 12 meatballs.

Heat the oil in a large skillet over medium-high heat. Add the meatballs and cook for 3 to 5 minutes, turning frequently, until golden brown on all sides. Add the sauce and bring to a simmer. Simmer for 5 minutes, or until the meatballs are cooked through.

Arrange a meatball and some sauce on each roll and serve.

Sweet-and-Sour Turkey Meatballs

Serves 4 ■ Prep time: 10 minutes ■ Cooking time: 10 minutes

The sweet-and-sour flavor comes from the happy marriage of tomato sauce, plum sauce, and cider vinegar. I also add a little chili powder for depth. Feel free to make the meatballs with lean ground beef if you like. For birthday parties, serve the meatballs on wooden picks. For larger groups, simply double or triple the recipe.

The meatballs can be made up to 3 days in advance and refrigerated until ready to reheat in a large saucepan. You can also freeze the cooked meatballs in the sauce for up to 3 months. Thaw completely in the refrigerator before reheating in a saucepan.

Nutrients per serving:
Calories: 299
Fat: 6g
Saturated Fat: <1g
Cholesterol: 34mg
Carbohydrate: 41g
Protein: 23g
Fiber: 2g
Sodium: 477mg

1 pound ground turkey
Salt and freshly ground black pepper
1 tablespoon canola oil
1 (15-ounce) can tomato sauce
1 cup plum sauce
2 tablespoons cider vinegar
1 teaspoon chili powder

In a large bowl, combine the ground turkey, about ¼ teaspoon salt, and about ¼ teaspoon pepper. Mix well and shape the mixture into 16 meatballs.

Heat the oil in a large skillet over medium-high heat. Add the meatballs and cook for 3 to 5 minutes, turning frequently, until golden brown on all sides. Meanwhile, in a small bowl, whisk together the tomato sauce, plum sauce, vinegar, and chili powder. Add the mixture to the pan and bring to a simmer. Simmer for 5 minutes, or until the meatballs are cooked through.

Shrimp & Tomato Calzone

Serves 4 ■ Prep time: 10 to 15 minutes ■ Cooking time: 20 to 25 minutes

Nutrients per serving:
Calories: 379
Fat: 9g
Saturated Fat: 3g
Cholesterol: 96mg
Carbohydrate: 54g
Protein: 25g
Fiber: 3g
Sodium: 601mg

If you think you can't pair shrimp and cheese, think again. They're awesome together, especially when combined with tomatoes and nestled inside pizza dough. For finicky eaters who don't eat shrimp, substitute 2 cups cubed or shredded cooked chicken or 1 cup cooked ground chicken or turkey.

The calzone can be assembled up to 24 hours in advance and refrigerated until ready to bake. You can also freeze the assembled calzone for up to 3 months. Thaw completely in the refrigerator before baking. For larger groups, simply double or triple the recipe and make multiple calzones.

Cooking spray

1 pound frozen bread dough, thawed according to package directions

8 ounces cooked medium shrimp, peeled, deveined, and halved crosswise

1 (14-ounce) can no-salt-added diced tomatoes

1 teaspoon salt-free Italian seasoning

⅔ cup shredded part-skim mozzarella cheese

Preheat the oven to 400°F. Coat a large baking sheet with cooking spray.

Roll the dough out into a large circle about ½ inch thick and 15 to 18 inches in diameter.

In a medium bowl, combine the shrimp, tomatoes, and Italian seasoning. Mix well. Spoon the mixture onto one half of the dough, to within ½ inch of the edges. Sprinkle the cheese over the shrimp mixture. Pull the untopped side of the dough up and over the filling and pinch the edges together to seal. Transfer the calzone to the prepared baking sheet and spray the surface of the calzone with cooking spray.

Bake for 20 to 25 minutes, until the calzone is puffed up and golden brown.

Cheddar Fondue with Shrimp & Apples

Serves 4 ■ Prep time: 10 minutes ■ Cooking time: 10 minutes

My mom made fondue all the time when I was growing up, especially when she threw dinner parties. In honor of her, I created this recipe, a sensational pot of melted cheese served with tender shrimp and tart apples. For variety, serve the fondue with cubed bread, grilled chicken, and assorted vegetables. For larger groups, simply double or triple the recipe.

Nutrients per serving:
Calories: 485
Fat: 23g
Saturated Fat: 13g
Cholesterol: 237mg
Carbohydrate: 25g
Protein: 42g
Fiber: 2g
Sodium: 631mg

8 ounces mild or sharp cheddar cheese, shredded, or a combination of the two

1 tablespoon cornstarch or all-purpose flour

1 (12-ounce) can evaporated skim milk

Salt and freshly ground black pepper

1 pound cooked large shrimp, peeled and deveined (tails on)

2 Granny Smith apples, cored and sliced

Combine the cheese and cornstarch in a large resealable bag and shake to coat the cheese with the cornstarch.

Heat the milk in a medium saucepan over medium heat. When tiny bubbles appear around the edges of the pan, gradually stir in the cheese. Simmer until the cheese melts and the mixture is smooth, stirring constantly. Remove from the heat and season to taste with salt and pepper.

Serve the fondue with the shrimp and apples on the side for dunking.

Shrimp & Yellow Squash Skewers

Serves 4 ■ Prep time: 10 to 15 minutes ■ Cooking time: 3 to 5 minutes

Black bean sauce is a rich, thick sauce made with fermented black beans and soy. It's an excellent addition to all types of skewered food. Look for black bean sauce with the Asian ingredients in the grocery store. I like to serve these skewers with rice or cellophane (bean thread/mung bean) noodles. To make the skewers finicky friendly, select an assortment of vegetables the whole family will enjoy.

The skewers can be assembled up to 24 hours in advance and refrigerated until ready to cook. When using wooden skewers, soak them in water for at least 10 minutes before using to prevent them from burning. You will need 8 to 10 skewers.

Nutrients per serving:
Calories: 156
Fat: 3g
Saturated Fat: <1g
Cholesterol: 172mg
Carbohydrate: 7g
Protein: 24g
Fiber: 1g
Sodium: 280mg

Cooking spray
1 pound large shrimp, peeled and deveined (tails on, if desired)
1 medium yellow summer squash, cut into 1-inch pieces
1 small red onion, cut into 2-inch pieces
16 to 20 cherry or grape tomatoes
Salt and freshly ground black pepper
¼ cup black bean sauce

Coat a stovetop grill pan or griddle with cooking spray and preheat over medium-high heat.

Skewer the shrimp, squash, onion, and tomatoes on metal or wooden skewers. Season the shrimp and vegetables with salt and pepper. Brush the black bean sauce all over the shrimp and vegetables.

Add the skewers to the hot pan and cook for 3 to 5 minutes, until the shrimp are opaque (cooked through) and the vegetables are crisp-tender.

Key West Po'boys with Lime & Mayo

Serves 4 ■ Prep time: 10 to 15 minutes

To make sure you really create a po'boy (poor boy) sandwich, look for a cooked shrimp variety that's on sale (or buy raw shrimp and cook it first). I love this sandwich because it's mildly tart from the lime and packed with flavor from the Caribbean seasoning. You can also use Old Bay or seafood seasoning. For added crunch, add one romaine lettuce leaf to each sandwich. And when you're ready to splurge a little bit, you may also make these sandwiches with cooked lobster meat.

The shrimp mixture can be made up to 24 hours in advance and refrigerated until ready to spoon onto the rolls. For larger groups, simply double or triple the recipe.

Nutrients per serving:
Calories: 293
Fat: 10g
Saturated Fat: 2g
Cholesterol: 179mg
Carbohydrate: 22g
Protein: 26g
Fiber: 1g
Sodium: 627mg

⅓ **cup light mayonnaise**
Juice and zest of 1 lime
1 teaspoon Caribbean seasoning (regular or salt-free)
1 pound cooked small or medium shrimp, peeled and deveined
Salt and freshly ground black pepper
4 soft French rolls

In a medium bowl, whisk together the mayonnaise, 1 tablespoon of the lime juice, 1 teaspoon of the lime zest, and the Caribbean seasoning. Fold in the shrimp. Season to taste with salt and pepper. Spoon the mixture onto the rolls and serve.

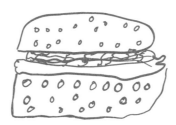

Seared Tilapia with Fresh Fruit Salsa

Serves 4 ■ Prep time: 15 minutes ■ Cooking time: 4 to 6 minutes

Because tilapia is a mild-flavored, white-fleshed fish, it comes to life when partnered with the tart flavors of pineapple and lime and sweet honeydew melon. You may also make the salsa with cantaloupe instead of honeydew. For a little heat, add a seeded and finely diced jalapeño pepper. The salsa also works very well with chicken and pork, for those who don't like fish.

1 cup finely diced honeydew melon

1 cup finely diced pineapple (fresh or canned in 100% juice)

2 tablespoons chopped fresh cilantro

Juice and zest of 1 lime

Salt and freshly ground black pepper

2 teaspoons canola oil

4 tilapia fillets (about 4 ounces each)

Nutrients per serving:
Calories: 165
Fat: 5g
Saturated Fat: 1g
Cholesterol: 49mg
Carbohydrate: 9g
Protein: 23g
Fiber: 1g
Sodium: 56mg

In a medium bowl, combine the melon, pineapple, cilantro, 1 tablespoon of the lime juice, and 1 teaspoon of the lime zest. Mix well. Season to taste with salt and pepper.

Heat the oil in a large skillet over medium-high heat. Season both sides of the tilapia with salt and pepper and add the fish to the hot pan. Cook for 2 to 3 minutes per side, until the fish is fork-tender. Serve the fish with the salsa spooned over the top.

Tilapia with Tomato-Zucchini Relish

Serves 4 ■ Prep time: 15 minutes ■ Cooking time: 4 to 6 minutes

Nutrients per serving:
Calories: 147
Fat: 5g
Saturated Fat: 1g
Cholesterol: 49mg
Carbohydrate: 4g
Protein: 23g
Fiber: 1g
Sodium: 54mg

Zucchini, tomatoes, and basil shout "summer," so take advantage of the season's best when they are available at the grocery store or farmers' market. You can also make the relish with yellow summer squash and green bell pepper instead of the zucchini.

The relish is also excellent with chicken and steak, so make a big batch. Store extra relish in the refrigerator for up to 4 days.

1½ cups finely diced tomatoes (beefsteak or plum)
1 small zucchini, finely diced
2 tablespoons chopped fresh basil
1 tablespoon cider vinegar
Salt and freshly ground black pepper
2 teaspoons olive oil
4 tilapia fillets (about 4 ounces each)

In a medium bowl, combine the tomatoes, zucchini, basil, and vinegar. Mix well. Season to taste with salt and pepper.

Heat the oil in a large skillet over medium-high heat. Season both sides of the tilapia with salt and pepper and add the fish to the hot pan. Cook for 2 to 3 minutes per side, until the fish is fork-tender. Serve the fish with the relish spooned over the top.

Salt-Baked Salmon with Olive Relish

Serves 4 ■ Prep time: 15 minutes ■ Cooking time: 15 minutes

When fish is baked in salt, it retains its moisture and is exceptionally flavorful. Chefs typically use red snapper, sea bass, or striped bass (whole fish that's been scaled and cleaned), but I like using salmon fillets so that the dish can go straight from the oven to the table. Get the kids involved in salting the fish—it's a messy and fun adventure!

2 cups coarse kosher salt

4 salmon fillets (about 4 ounces each)

Freshly ground black pepper

¼ cup chopped pimento-stuffed olives

2 tablespoons chopped fresh parsley

2 tablespoons chopped scallions (white and green parts)

Nutrients per serving:

Calories: 167

Fat: 10g

Saturated Fat: 2g

Cholesterol: 52mg

Carbohydrate: 1g

Protein: 17g

Fiber: 1g

Sodium: 605mg

Preheat the oven to 400°F.

In a medium bowl, combine the salt and ¼ cup water. Mix until you create a "wet sand" consistency, adding up to ¼ cup more water if necessary. Spread a thin layer of the salt mixture in the bottom of a shallow baking dish. Arrange the salmon fillets, skin side down, on top of the salt. Season the top of the salmon with the pepper. Press the remaining salt all over the top and sides of the salmon. Bake for 15 minutes (you can't check for doneness when the fish is crusted with salt).

Meanwhile, in a small bowl, combine the olives, parsley, and scallions. Mix well.

Remove the fish from the oven and chip away the top salt crust (the skin should peel away along with the bottom layer of salt). Transfer the salmon to a serving platter and top with the olive relish.

Grilled Salmon with Ginger–Sweet Onion Vinaigrette

Serves 4 ■ Prep time: 5 to 10 minutes ■ Cooking time: 4 to 6 minutes

Nutrients per serving:
Calories: 263
Fat: 13g
Saturated Fat: 2g
Cholesterol: 52mg
Carbohydrate: 20g
Protein: 17g
Fiber: 1g
Sodium: 337mg

I chose to embellish store-bought, light honey mustard vinaigrette for this recipe, kicking up the flavors with sweet onion, ginger, and chives. If you have a particular vinaigrette-style dressing you know your family will love, you may certainly substitute that. To please finicky eaters, this dish can also be made with shrimp, scallops, tilapia, snapper, or halibut. And, of course, there's always chicken. . . .

Cooking spray

4 salmon fillets (about 4 ounces each)

Salt and freshly ground black pepper

1 cup light honey mustard vinaigrette or dressing

¼ cup chopped yellow or Vidalia onion

2 teaspoons minced fresh ginger

2 tablespoons chopped fresh chives

Coat a stovetop grill pan or griddle with cooking spray and preheat over medium-high heat. Season both sides of the salmon with salt and pepper and add the fish to the hot pan. Cook for 2 to 3 minutes per side, until the fish is fork-tender (still pink in the center is also fine).

Meanwhile, in a blender, combine the vinaigrette, onion, and ginger. Puree until blended. Transfer the mixture to a bowl and stir in the chives.

Arrange the salmon on a serving platter and spoon the vinaigrette over the top.

Honey-Pecan Baked Salmon

Serves 4 ■ Prep time: 10 minutes ■ Cooking time: 15 to 20 minutes

Kids love the nutty crunch of this salmon coating. The first layer is a sweet and tangy blend of mustard and honey, followed by a layer of crisp panko bread crumbs and pecans. You can also make the same coating with walnuts or almonds and, instead of salmon, use it on boneless, skinless chicken breasts.

Cooking spray
4 salmon fillets (about 4 ounces each)
Salt and freshly ground black pepper
3 tablespoons honey
2 teaspoons Dijon mustard
½ cup finely chopped pecans
2 tablespoons panko (Japanese bread crumbs)

Nutrients per serving:
Calories: 322
Fat: 21g
Saturated Fat: 3g
Cholesterol: 52mg
Carbohydrate: 18g
Protein: 19g
Fiber: 2g
Sodium: 106mg

Preheat the oven to 375°F. Coat a shallow baking dish with cooking spray.

Arrange the salmon in the prepared baking dish, skin side down, and season the top with salt and pepper.

In a small bowl, whisk together the honey and mustard. Spread the mixture all over the top and sides of the salmon.

In another small bowl, combine the pecans and panko. Mix well. Press the pecan mixture into the top and sides of the salmon. Bake for 15 to 20 minutes, until the salmon is fork-tender.

Salmon-Dill Cakes with Mustard-Yogurt Sauce

Serves 4 ■ Prep time: 10 to 15 minutes ■ Cooking time: 10 minutes

These cakes are light and flavorful thanks to the blend of salmon, Greek yogurt, and fresh dill. Once cooked, they're nestled under a zesty, thick yogurt-mustard sauce. You can also make these cakes with light tuna (packed in water) or fresh lump crabmeat. Oftentimes salmon cakes (and other fish cakes, such as tuna or crab) fall apart while they cook, so for the best results, I like to refrigerate the cakes for at least 15 minutes before cooking.

You can assemble the cakes up to 24 hours in advance and refrigerate them until ready to cook; same goes for the mustard-yogurt sauce.

Nutrients per serving:
Calories: 214
Fat: 11g
Saturated Fat: 2g
Cholesterol: 55mg
Carbohydrate: 8g
Protein: 21g
Fiber: <1g
Sodium: 150mg

12 ounces cooked salmon (canned or fillets)
1 cup low-fat plain Greek yogurt
¼ cup panko (Japanese bread crumbs)
2 tablespoons chopped fresh dill
Salt and freshly ground black pepper
Cooking spray
2 teaspoons Dijon mustard

In a medium bowl, combine the salmon, ⅓ cup of the yogurt, the panko, dill, and salt and pepper to taste. Mix well and shape the mixture into 4 equal patties, each about 1 inch thick.

Coat a stovetop griddle or large skillet with cooking spray and preheat over medium-high heat. Add the salmon cakes to the hot pan and cook for 3 to 5 minutes per side, until golden brown and heated through (do not flip more than once, as the cakes are too delicate for multiple flips).

Meanwhile, in a small bowl, whisk together the remaining ⅔ cup yogurt and the mustard. Serve the salmon cakes with the yogurt-mustard sauce drizzled over the top.

Salmon Niçoise with Warm Green Beans, Potatoes & Mustard Vinaigrette

Serves 4 ■ Prep time: 15 minutes ■ Cooking time: 15 minutes

The recipe title says it all—warm salmon salad with tender potatoes, crisp-tender green beans, and a flavor-packed, mustard-based vinaigrette. You can also make the dish with tuna (substitute steaks for the salmon, or use canned and start at step 3) or grilled chicken breasts. To make sure the dish is gluten-free, check the label on the salad dressing.

Nutrients per serving:
Calories: 301
Fat: 12g
Saturated Fat: 2g
Cholesterol: 52mg
Carbohydrate: 30g
Protein: 21g
Fiber: 4g
Sodium: 197mg

Cooking spray
4 salmon fillets (about 4 ounces each)
Salt and freshly ground black pepper
2 large or 3 medium Yukon gold potatoes, cut into 2-inch pieces
2 cups green beans, ends trimmed
½ cup light honey mustard vinaigrette or dressing
4 cups chopped romaine lettuce

Preheat the oven to 400°F. Coat a large baking sheet with cooking spray.

Season both sides of the salmon with salt and pepper and place the salmon on the prepared baking sheet. Bake for 15 minutes, or until the salmon is fork-tender. Set aside.

Meanwhile, place the potatoes in a large saucepan and pour over enough cold water to cover by 2 inches. Set the pan over high heat and bring to a boil. Boil for 9 minutes. Add the green beans and boil for 1 more minute, until the potatoes are fork-tender and the green beans are crisp-tender. Drain and transfer the potatoes and green beans to a large bowl. Add the dressing and stir to coat.

Remove the skin from the salmon fillets and break the salmon into chunks. Add the salmon to the potato mixture and stir gently to combine. Season to taste with salt and pepper.

Arrange the lettuce on a serving platter. Spoon the salmon and potato mixture over the top.

Crab Cakes with Creamy Broccoli Slaw

Serves 4 ■ Prep time: 15 minutes ■ Cooking time: 10 minutes

I love nestling these crab cakes over or under the creamy-and-crunchy broccoli slaw. Look for broccoli slaw next to the other coleslaw mixes at the grocery store. You can also substitute regular coleslaw if you prefer. Sometimes I jazz up the tartar sauce with extra pickle relish or diced pickled jalapeño peppers. For birthday parties, make 10 to 12 mini crab cakes and serve them with or without the slaw. For larger groups, simply double or triple the recipe.

The crab cakes hold their shape better when refrigerated for about 15 minutes before cooking. You can assemble the crab cakes and slaw up to 24 hours in advance and refrigerate them until ready to cook.

Nutrients per serving:

Calories: 169

Fat: 3g

Saturated Fat: 0g

Cholesterol: 66mg

Carbohydrate: 17g

Protein: 19g

Fiber: 3g

Sodium: 792mg

¾ cup light tartar sauce

¼ cup plain dry bread crumbs

12 ounces fresh lump crabmeat

Salt and freshly ground black pepper

Cooking spray

1 (12-ounce) bag broccoli slaw (broccoli, carrots, and cabbage)

2 tablespoons cider vinegar

In a large bowl, combine ¼ cup of the tartar sauce and the bread crumbs. Mix well. Gently fold in the crabmeat. Season to taste with salt and pepper. Shape the mixture into 4 equal patties, each about 1 inch thick.

Coat a stovetop griddle or large skillet with cooking spray and preheat over medium-high heat. Add the crab cakes to the hot pan and cook for 3 to 5 minutes per side, until golden brown and heated through (do not flip more than once, as the cakes are too delicate for multiple flips).

Meanwhile, in a large bowl, combine the slaw mix, the remaining ½ cup tartar sauce, and the vinegar. Mix well. Season to taste with salt and pepper.

Serve the crab cakes with the slaw (on top or underneath).

Grilled Tuna with White Peach Salsa

Serves 4 ■ Prep time: 10 to 15 minutes ■ Cooking time: 4 to 6 minutes

Nutrients per serving:
Calories: 191
Fat: 6g
Saturated Fat: 1g
Cholesterol: 42mg
Carbohydrate: 8g
Protein: 26g
Fiber: 1g
Sodium: 43mg

This sweet peach salsa is also excellent over grilled chicken or pork. You may also make the salsa with regular yellow peaches (fresh or thawed frozen) or nectarines. For finicky palates, substitute parsley for the cilantro or leave out the herb altogether. You can do the same with the white onion.

Cooking spray
4 tuna steaks (about 4 ounces each)
Salt and freshly ground black pepper
2 cups diced white peaches
¼ cup finely diced white onion
Juice and zest of 1 lime
2 tablespoons chopped fresh cilantro

Coat a stovetop grill pan or griddle with cooking spray and preheat over medium-high heat.

Season both sides of the tuna steaks with salt and pepper. Add the tuna steaks to the hot pan and cook for 2 to 3 minutes per side, until the fish is fork-tender.

Meanwhile, in a medium bowl, combine the peaches, onion, 1 tablespoon of the lime juice, 2 teaspoons of the lime zest, and the cilantro. Mix well. Season to taste with salt and pepper.

Serve the tuna with the salsa spooned over the top.

Braised Tuna with Mango, Jicama & Watercress

Serves 4 ■ Prep time: 5 to 10 minutes ■ Cooking time: 5 minutes

Jicama is a unique, crunchy vegetable that tastes like a cross between a potato and an apple. The crisp texture and subtle sweetness partner perfectly with the tender mango and peppery watercress. For finicky eaters, substitute baby spinach for the watercress (when I was little, I despised watercress for some reason; I could smell it a mile away).

Nutrients per serving:
Calories: 289
Fat: 9g
Saturated Fat: 2g
Cholesterol: 42mg
Carbohydrate: 22g
Protein: 27g
Fiber: 3g
Sodium: 53mg

1 tablespoon canola oil
4 tuna steaks (about 4 ounces each)
Salt and freshly ground black pepper
2 cups diced mango
1 cup diced peeled jicama
2 cups watercress leaves
¼ cup mirin (Japanese rice wine)

Heat the oil in a large skillet over medium-high heat. Season both sides of the tuna steaks with salt and pepper. Add the tuna to the hot pan and cook for 1 minute per side, until golden brown. Add the mango and jicama and cook for 2 minutes, or until the mango softens and releases liquid. Add the watercress and mirin and bring to a simmer. Simmer for 1 minute, until the watercress leaves wilt and the tuna is fork-tender.

Serve the tuna steaks with the mango, jicama, and watercress mixture spooned over the top.

Seared Tuna with Oranges, Avocado & Cilantro

Serves 4 ■ Prep time: 5 to 10 minutes ■ Cooking time: 5 minutes

Finicky eaters love the sweet and salty combination of the oranges, soy sauce, and creamy avocado. Plus, avocado is packed with the nutrients kids need for their developing brains. You can also make the dish with boneless, skinless chicken breasts instead of the tuna.

Nutrients per serving:
Calories: 302
Fat: 16g
Saturated Fat: 3g
Cholesterol: 42mg
Carbohydrate: 12g
Protein: 27g
Fiber: 4g
Sodium: 245mg

1 tablespoon canola oil

4 tuna steaks (about 4 ounces each)

Salt and freshly ground black pepper

1 (11-ounce) can mandarin oranges in juice, undrained

2 tablespoons reduced-sodium soy sauce

1 ripe avocado, pitted, peeled, and diced

2 tablespoons chopped fresh cilantro

Heat the oil in a large skillet over medium-high heat. Season both sides of the tuna steaks with salt and pepper. Add the tuna to the hot pan and cook for 1 minute per side, until golden brown. Add the oranges and juice from the can and the soy sauce and bring to a simmer. Simmer for 2 minutes, or until the tuna is fork-tender.

Arrange the tuna on a serving platter, spoon over the oranges and soy sauce mixture, and top with the avocado and cilantro.

Individual Meat Loaf "Cupcakes" with Creamy Ketchup "Icing"

Serves 6 ■ Prep time: 10 to 15 minutes ■ Cooking time: 25 to 30 minutes

A typical one-pan meat loaf takes about an hour to bake. But by pressing the mixture into muffin cups instead of a loaf pan, the cooking time is slashed in half! And I simply jazzed up the beef by adding seasoned Italian bread crumbs to the mini loaves before topping them with sour cream–spiked ketchup. To add vegetables to the meat loaf, stir in 1 cup finely diced carrots and ½ cup finely diced celery or bell pepper.

The meat loaf "cupcakes" can be assembled up to 24 hours in advance and refrigerated until ready to bake. For larger groups, simply double or triple the recipe and fill more muffin cups.

Cooking spray
1 pound lean ground beef
⅓ cup Italian-style dry bread crumbs
1 large egg
Salt and freshly ground black pepper
½ cup ketchup
2 tablespoons light sour cream

Preheat the oven to 350°F. Coat a 6-cup muffin pan with cooking spray.

In a large bowl, combine the ground beef, bread crumbs, egg, about ¼ teaspoon salt, and about ¼ teaspoon pepper. Mix well. Press the mixture into the prepared muffin pan.

In a small bowl, whisk together the ketchup and sour cream. Spread the mixture over the meat loaf cakes.

Bake for 25 to 30 minutes, until the meat loaf is cooked through (the loaf will have pulled away from the sides of the pan and the internal temperature will be at least 165°F).

Grilled Steak Lettuce Wraps

Serves 4 ■ Prep time: 5 minutes ■ Cooking time: 10 minutes
Resting time: 10 minutes

Liquid smoke is a hickory- or mesquite-flavored seasoning sold with the barbecue sauce in the grocery store. It's excellent on steak. To make the wraps, I like using Bibb or baby lettuce leaves because they're tender and roll up easily. You can also use romaine lettuce leaves or flour or corn tortillas. When I make these at home, I often serve diced avocado, jalapeño slices, and banana peppers on the side. You may also prepare this with chicken or tofu and add your favorite wrap or taco fillings.

Nutrients per serving:
Calories: 284
Fat: 16g
Saturated Fat: 9g
Cholesterol: 63mg
Carbohydrate: 4g
Protein: 31g
Fiber: 1g
Sodium: 252mg

Cooking spray
1 pound flank steak
Salt and freshly ground black pepper
2 teaspoons liquid smoke
12 Bibb or baby lettuce leaves
1 cup diced tomato (beefsteak or plum)
1 cup shredded Mexican cheese blend or sharp cheddar cheese

Coat a stovetop grill pan with cooking spray and preheat over medium-high heat. Season both sides of the steak with salt and pepper. Brush the liquid smoke all over both sides of the steak. Add the steak to the hot pan and cook for 5 minutes per side for medium doneness (pink in the center), or longer if desired. Remove the steak from the heat and let stand for 10 minutes.

Slice the steak across the grain into ¼-inch-thick strips.

Fill the lettuce leaves with the steak, tomato, and cheese, and roll up.

Sirloin Kebabs with Bell Peppers & Teriyaki

Serves 4 ■ Prep time: 10 to 15 minutes ■ Cooking time: 5 minutes

This is a finicky friendly dish because you can put any variety of vegetables on the skewer before brushing everything with the teriyaki sauce. You can also replace the steak with chicken or shrimp. I typically serve my skewers over rice or cellophane noodles that I've tossed with a little sesame oil and soy sauce.

The kebabs can be assembled up to 24 hours in advance and refrigerated until ready to cook. Soak wooden skewers in water for at least 10 minutes before using to prevent them from burning. You will need 8 to 10 skewers.

Nutrients per serving:
Calories: 188
Fat: 5g
Saturated Fat: 2g
Cholesterol: 47mg
Carbohydrate: 8g
Protein: 27g
Fiber: 2g
Sodium: 307mg

Cooking spray
1 pound sirloin steak, cut into 2-inch pieces
1 green bell pepper, seeded and cut into 2-inch pieces
1 red bell pepper, seeded and cut into 2-inch pieces
1 medium red onion, cut into 2-inch pieces
Salt and freshly ground black pepper
¼ cup reduced-sodium teriyaki sauce

Coat a stovetop grill pan or griddle with cooking spray and preheat over medium-high heat.

Skewer pieces of steak, bell pepper, and onion on metal or wooden skewers. Season the steak and vegetables with salt and pepper. Brush the teriyaki sauce all over the steak and vegetables.

Add the skewers to the hot pan and cook for about 5 minutes, or until the steak is medium (pink in the center) and the vegetables are crisp-tender, turning frequently. Cook longer for more fully cooked meat, if desired.

Roast Beef Chimichangas with Green Chiles & Cheddar

Serves 8 ■ Prep time: 15 minutes ■ Cooking time: 15 minutes

Chimichangas are deep-fried burritos typically stuffed with rice, chicken, and cheese. Easy for a restaurant chef, not for a home cook. I stuff my chimichangas with refried beans, roast beef, cheese, and chiles, and then I bake them in the oven. Clearly, I like to mix up my ingredients, turning ordinary dishes into extraordinary meals. This dish is perfect for finicky eaters because you can put whatever filling you prefer into each individual chimichanga. And if you want to add a topping, try light sour cream and/or salsa.

The chimichangas can be assembled up to 24 hours in advance and refrigerated until ready to bake. For larger groups, simply double or triple the recipe.

Cooking spray
1 (14-ounce) can refried beans (regular or vegetarian)
4 ounces sharp cheddar cheese, shredded
1 (4-ounce) can chopped green chiles
8 fajita-size flour tortillas (regular or whole wheat)
8 ounces thinly sliced roast beef

Preheat the oven to 375°F. Coat a shallow baking dish with cooking spray.

In a large bowl, combine the refried beans, cheese, and green chiles. Mix well. Arrange the tortillas on a flat surface. Spoon an equal amount of the bean mixture in a rectangle onto the center of each tortilla. Top the filling with the roast beef. Fold over one side of a tortilla (near the long side of the rectangle of filling), covering the filling. Fold in the sides near the filling ends and finish rolling up. Repeat with the remaining tortillas. Place the chimichangas in the prepared pan and spray the surface of the chimichangas with cooking spray.

Bake for 15 minutes, or until the tortillas are golden brown.

Wok-Seared Beef with Orange & Teriyaki

Serves 4 ■ Prep time: 5 to 10 minutes ■ Cooking time: 5 minutes

Wok cooking is one of the fastest ways to go on a busy weeknight. In this dish, flavors soar thanks to the addition of ginger, garlic, mandarin oranges, and teriyaki sauce. I often serve this dish over Asian somen noodles or Chinese egg noodles. If you need veggie inspiration for future meals, the best vegetables to serve with this dish are bell peppers, zucchini, yellow summer squash, broccoli, bok choy, carrots, snap peas, and red onion. You can mix and match ingredients to suit every finicky family member.

Nutrients per serving:
Calories: 225
Fat: 9g
Saturated Fat: 2g
Cholesterol: 47mg
Carbohydrate: 10g
Protein: 26g
Fiber: 1g
Sodium: 316mg

1 tablespoon canola oil

1 pound lean steak, cut into thin strips

1 tablespoon minced fresh ginger

2 to 3 cloves garlic, minced

1 (11-ounce) can mandarin oranges in juice, undrained

¼ cup reduced-sodium teriyaki sauce

Salt and freshly ground black pepper

Heat the oil in a wok or large skillet over medium-high heat. Add the steak, ginger, and garlic and cook for 3 minutes, or until the steak is cooked to medium, stirring constantly. Add the oranges with the juice from the can and the teriyaki sauce and bring to a simmer. Simmer for 2 minutes to heat through. Remove the pan from the heat and season to taste with salt and pepper.

Grilled Steak Caprese Salad

Serves 4 ■ Prep time: 5 minutes ■ Cooking time: 10 minutes
Resting time: 10 minutes

Caprese salad is an Italian salad that typically consists of the freshest tomatoes, basil, and mozzarella you can find, drizzled with good-quality olive oil. Since I can't leave well enough alone, I decided to add delectable sliced steak! You can cut up a large ball of fresh mozzarella or buy the small fresh mozzarella balls (called bocconcini) that are packaged in water and sold with the other fresh cheeses (typically in the produce department or deli). Thick balsamic glaze is also a nice addition—drizzle a little over the top when you drizzle over the olive oil.

Nutrients per serving:
Calories: 365
Fat: 22g
Saturated Fat: 10g
Cholesterol: 86mg
Carbohydrate: 5g
Protein: 37g
Fiber: 1g
Sodium: 409mg

Cooking spray
1 pound flank or skirt steak
Salt and freshly ground black pepper
2 beefsteak tomatoes, cut into 1-inch pieces
8 ounces fresh mozzarella cheese, cut into 1-inch pieces
¼ cup torn fresh basil leaves
2 teaspoons olive oil

Coat a stovetop grill pan with cooking spray and preheat over medium-high heat. Season both sides of the steak with salt and pepper. Add the steak to the hot pan and cook for 5 minutes per side for medium doneness (pink in the center), or longer if desired. Remove the steak from the heat and let stand for 10 minutes.

Slice the steak across the grain into ¼-inch-thick strips.

Arrange the steak on a serving platter. Top the steak with the tomatoes, mozzarella, and basil. Drizzle the olive oil over the top.

Grilled Flank Steak with Blackberry Sauce

Serves 4 ■ Prep time: 5 minutes ■ Cooking time: 10 minutes
Resting time: 10 minutes

This sauce is ideal for finicky eaters because it's sweet from the blackberry preserves and tangy from the soy sauce and mustard. You may instead use raspberry or strawberry preserves or orange marmalade. And if you don't like seeds in your sauce, simply strain the sauce through a fine-mesh sieve, or buy seedless preserves. The sauce is also great spooned over chicken or pork.

Cooking spray
1 pound flank or skirt steak
Salt and freshly ground black pepper
1 cup blackberry preserves
2 tablespoons reduced-sodium soy sauce
1 teaspoon Dijon mustard

Coat a stovetop grill pan with cooking spray and preheat over medium-high heat. Season both sides of the steak with salt and pepper. Add the steak to the hot pan and cook for 5 minutes per side for medium doneness (pink in the center), or longer if desired. Remove the steak from the heat and let stand for 10 minutes.

Slice the steak across the grain into ¼-inch-thick strips.

Meanwhile, in a small saucepan, combine the blackberry preserves, soy sauce, and mustard. Mix well and set the pan over medium heat. Bring to a simmer, and then simmer for 5 minutes.

Arrange the steak on a serving platter and spoon the blackberry sauce over the top.

Southwestern Braised Short Ribs

Serves 4 ■ Prep time: 10 to 15 minutes ■ Cooking time: 2 hours

I put the birthday party icon with this recipe because my mom made ribs for my birthday every year when I was little! I love eating with my hands, and I adore the Southwest seasoning (typically a blend of chili powder, cumin, and other warming spices) in the sauce. The dish is jam-packed with flavor, and it's messy and fun for everyone. For larger groups, simply double or triple the recipe.

The ribs can be baked in advance and reheated just before serving. Store them in the refrigerator and reheat in the same Dutch oven over medium heat.

Nutrients per serving:
Calories: 409
Fat: 35g
Saturated Fat: 14g
Cholesterol: 65mg
Carbohydrate: 9g
Protein: 15g
Fiber: 2g
Sodium: 580mg

2 pounds short ribs
Salt and freshly ground black pepper
2 tablespoons salt-free Southwest seasoning
2 tablespoons all-purpose flour
1 tablespoon canola oil
1 (14-ounce) can tomato sauce
1 cup reduced-sodium beef broth

Preheat the oven to 375°F.

Season the ribs all over with salt and pepper. Season all over with the Southwest seasoning and then dust the ribs with the flour.

Heat the oil in a large Dutch oven or ovenproof pot over medium-high heat. Add the ribs and cook for 2 to 3 minutes, until browned on both sides. Add the tomato sauce and beef broth and bring to a simmer. Remove the pan from the heat, cover with a lid, and transfer to the oven. Bake for 2 hours, until the ribs are tender.

Sicilian Meatballs

Serves 4 ■ Prep time: 10 minutes ■ Cooking time: 20 minutes

The flavors of Italy abound in this dish thanks to the tomato sauce, fresh basil, and Parmesan cheese. I typically make this meal with beef, but you can also make the meatballs with ground turkey or chicken. To make this a complete meal, I usually serve the meatballs and sauce over cooked pasta or rice. For birthday parties, serve the meatballs on wooden picks. For larger groups, simply double or triple the recipe.

The meatballs can be made up to 3 days in advance and refrigerated until ready to reheat in a large saucepan. You can also freeze the cooked meatballs in the sauce for up to 3 months. Thaw completely in the refrigerator before reheating in a saucepan.

Nutrients per serving:
Calories: 214
Fat: 8g
Saturated Fat: 2.5g
Cholesterol: 47mg
Carbohydrate: 18g
Protein: 21g
Fiber: 4g
Sodium: 143mg

1 pound lean ground beef

2 teaspoons salt-free Italian seasoning

Salt and freshly ground black pepper

1 tablespoon olive oil

1 (28-ounce) can no-salt-added pureed tomatoes

¼ cup chopped fresh basil

2 tablespoons grated Parmesan cheese, plus more as desired for garnish

In a large bowl, combine the beef, seasoning, about ¼ teaspoon salt, and about ¼ teaspoon pepper. Mix well and shape the mixture into 16 meatballs.

Heat the oil in a large skillet over medium-high heat. Add the meatballs and cook for 5 to 7 minutes, turning frequently, until browned on all sides. Add the tomatoes and bring to a simmer. Decrease the heat to medium and simmer for 5 to 7 minutes, until the meatballs are cooked through. Stir in the basil and Parmesan and cook for 1 minute, until the cheese melts.

Transfer the meatballs to a serving platter and garnish with extra Parmesan, if desired.

Roasted Pork Tenderloin with Berry-Almond Salad

Serves 4 ■ Prep time: 10 minutes ■ Cooking time: 25 minutes
Standing time: 10 minutes

Mild pork comes to life in this dish thanks to the addition of fresh fruit, lemon, and mint. You can make the dish finicky friendly by choosing any berry or fruit blend you prefer. I don't recommend frozen fruit here, so if fresh berries aren't in season, make the salad with apples, pears, or peaches instead.

Nutrients per serving:
Calories: 196
Fat: 7g
Saturated Fat: 1g
Cholesterol: 62mg
Carbohydrate: 9g
Protein: 25g
Fiber: 4g
Sodium: 49mg

Cooking spray
1 pound pork tenderloin
Salt and freshly ground black pepper
⅓ cup sliced blanched almonds
2 cups mixed fresh berries (raspberries, strawberries, and/or blackberries)
Juice and zest of 1 lemon
1 tablespoon minced fresh mint

Preheat the oven to 400°F. Coat a shallow baking dish with cooking spray.

Season the pork all over with salt and pepper and place in the prepared baking dish. Roast for 20 to 25 minutes, until an instant-read thermometer inserted in the center reads 145°F. Remove the pork from the oven and let stand for 10 minutes.

Meanwhile, place the almonds in a small dry skillet over medium heat. Cook for 3 to 5 minutes, shaking the skillet frequently, until the almonds are golden brown.

Transfer the almonds to a medium bowl, add the berries, 1 tablespoon of the lemon juice, 1 teaspoon of the lemon zest, and the mint. Stir to combine.

Slice the pork crosswise into 1-inch-thick rounds and spoon the berry salad over the top.

Grilled Pork Chops with Sea Salt–Vinegar Slaw

Serves 4 ■ Prep time: 10 minutes ■ Cooking time: 15 minutes

Nutrients per serving:
Calories: 261
Fat: 12g
Saturated Fat: 4g
Cholesterol: 71mg
Carbohydrate: 15g
Protein: 23g
Fiber: 3g
Sodium: 570mg

The inspiration for this slaw came from one of my favorite snacks: sea salt and vinegar potato chips. This slaw is clearly a healthier option. And for the perfect balance of sweet and tart flavors, I combine vinegar and salt with a little honey. For variety, broccoli slaw mix, shredded red cabbage, and shredded carrots (all on their own) make excellent alternatives to regular coleslaw mix.

The slaw can be made up to 24 hours in advance and refrigerated until ready to serve.

Cooking spray
4 boneless pork loin chops (about 4 ounces each)
Salt and freshly ground black pepper
¼ cup cider vinegar
2 tablespoons honey
1 teaspoon sea salt
1 (16-ounce) package coleslaw mix

Coat a stovetop grill pan with cooking spray and preheat over medium-high heat. Season both sides of the pork chops with salt and pepper. Add the chops to the hot pan and cook for 3 to 5 minutes per side, until golden brown and still slightly pink in the center.

Meanwhile, in a large bowl, whisk together the vinegar, honey, and sea salt. Stir in the coleslaw mix and mix well. Season to taste with black pepper.

Serve the pork chops with the slaw on the side.

Grilled Pork & Pear Salad with Goat Cheese & Pecans

Serves 4 ■ Prep time: 10 minutes ■ Cooking time: 10 minutes

Nutrients per serving:
Calories: 338
Fat: 17g
Saturated Fat: 6g
Cholesterol: 93mg
Carbohydrate: 15g
Protein: 31g
Fiber: 5g
Sodium: 99mg

The pear mixture is a flavor-packed blend of sweet pears, salty goat cheese, crunchy pecans, and white balsamic vinegar. And since pork has a natural affinity with fruit, the ensemble is spot-on. For added flavor and color, add 2 tablespoons chopped fresh parsley to the pear mixture. Make the dish finicky friendly by substituting your favorite nut (such as walnuts or almonds) for the pecans. Some kids also prefer feta cheese to goat cheese. You may also serve the pear mixture over grilled or roasted chicken breasts.

Cooking spray

1 pound pork tenderloin, cut crosswise into 1-inch-thick rounds

Salt and freshly ground black pepper

4 pears, cored and diced (peeled, if desired)

⅓ cup crumbled goat cheese (plain or seasoned)

⅓ cup pecan pieces

1 tablespoon white balsamic vinegar

Coat a stovetop grill pan with cooking spray and preheat over medium-high heat. Season both sides of the pork slices with salt and pepper. Add the pork to the hot pan and cook for 3 minutes per side, until golden brown and still slightly pink in the center.

Meanwhile, in a medium bowl, combine the pears, goat cheese, pecans, and balsamic vinegar. Stir to combine.

Arrange the pork slices on a serving platter and top with the pear mixture.

Wok-Seared Pork with Pineapple, Bell Peppers & Ginger

Serves 4 ■ Prep time: 10 minutes ■ Cooking time: 10 minutes

You'll adore the combination of ingredients in this fast meal: tart pineapple, sweet red peppers, pungent ginger, and salty hoisin sauce. I like to serve this mixture over fluffy couscous, either the regular variety or the larger Israeli couscous. Make the dish finicky friendly and add your family's favorite vegetables. The dish can also be made with chicken or shrimp.

Nutrients per serving:
Calories: 262
Fat: 10g
Saturated Fat: 2g
Cholesterol: 80mg
Carbohydrate: 16g
Protein: 27g
Fiber: 2g
Sodium: 317mg

1 tablespoon canola oil

1 pound pork tenderloin, cut into 1-inch pieces

1 tablespoon minced fresh ginger

2 bell peppers (preferably 1 green and 1 red), seeded and chopped

1 cup cubed pineapple (fresh or canned in 100% juice)

¼ cup hoisin sauce

Salt and freshly ground black pepper

Heat the oil in a wok or large skillet over medium-high heat. Add the pork and cook for 3 minutes, stirring frequently, until golden brown on all sides. Add the ginger and cook for 1 minute, until the ginger is fragrant. Add the bell peppers, pineapple, and hoisin sauce and cook for 2 minutes, stirring frequently, until the peppers are crisp-tender. Season to taste with salt and pepper.

Pork Chops with Apple Tartar Sauce

Serves 4 ■ Prep time: 10 minutes ■ Cooking time: 10 minutes

This sweetened-up version of tartar sauce makes this a great dish for kids. I chose McIntosh apples for this salad because they have a nice balance of sweet and tart flavors. You may also use Fuji, Gala, Granny Smith, Red Delicious, or your favorite apple variety. You can also serve the sauce over chicken or fish.

Nutrients per serving:
Calories: 284
Fat: 13g
Saturated Fat: 4g
Cholesterol: 71mg
Carbohydrate: 17g
Protein: 22g
Fiber: 1g
Sodium: 579mg

Cooking spray
4 boneless pork loin chops (about 4 ounces each)
Salt and freshly ground black pepper
¾ cup light tartar sauce
1 McIntosh apple, peeled, cored, and finely diced
Juice and zest of 1 lemon
1 tablespoon minced fresh chives

Coat a stovetop grill pan with cooking spray and preheat over medium-high heat. Season both sides of the pork chops with salt and pepper. Add the chops to the hot pan and cook for 3 minutes per side, until golden brown and still slightly pink in the center.

Meanwhile, in a medium bowl, combine the tartar sauce, apple, 2 teaspoons of the lemon juice, 1 teaspoon of the lemon zest, and the chives. Mix well.

Arrange the pork chops on a serving platter and spoon the tartar sauce over the top.

Savory Bread Pudding with Ham & Sun-Dried Tomatoes

Serves 4 ■ Prep time: 10 to 15 minutes ■ Cooking time: 45 minutes

Nutrients per serving:
Calories: 321
Fat: 10g
Saturated Fat: 3g
Cholesterol: 112mg
Carbohydrate: 38g
Protein: 19g
Fiber: 3g
Sodium: 450mg

This make-ahead-friendly bread pudding is the perfect addition to a brunch birthday celebration. Sweet sun-dried tomatoes and salty ham add terrific flavor to the bread and milk base. For even more flavor, sprinkle 1 to 2 tablespoons of grated Parmesan cheese over the bread pudding just before baking. For finicky eaters, you may substitute smoked turkey for the ham and use your favorite bread variety.

The bread pudding can be assembled up to 24 hours in advance and refrigerated until ready to bake. For larger groups, simply double or triple the recipe and make two to three bread puddings.

Cooking spray
8 slices bread (preferably low-sodium, day-old, whole grain white or wheat)
1 cup diced low-sodium baked ham
1 cup diced oil-packed sun-dried tomatoes
2 cups low-fat (1%) milk
2 large eggs
Salt and freshly ground black pepper

Preheat the oven to 350°F. Coat an 8-inch square baking dish with cooking spray.

Break the bread into small pieces and arrange in the bottom of the prepared baking dish. Arrange the ham and sun-dried tomatoes on top of the bread.

In a medium bowl, whisk together the milk, eggs, ¼ teaspoon salt, and ¼ teaspoon pepper. Pour the milk mixture over the bread, ham, and sun-dried tomatoes. Push down with a fork to make sure the bread is covered and soaking up the egg mixture.

Bake for 45 minutes, or until the top is browned and springs back when lightly tapped.

Mustard-Glazed Ham Steaks with Raspberry Sauce

Serves 4 ■ Prep time: 5 minutes ■ Cooking time: 10 minutes

Nutrients per serving:
Calories: 152
Fat: 4g
Saturated Fat: <1g
Cholesterol: 26mg
Carbohydrate: 19g
Protein: 13g
Fiber: 5g
Sodium: 785mg

Ham steaks are fully cooked, thick-cut ham slices that make a quick and delicious meal. I like to brush the steaks with honey mustard, grill them, and then drizzle a sweet raspberry sauce over the top. This dish takes an ordinary ham steak and turns it into a dazzling main course. For finicky eaters, strain the raspberry sauce through a fine-mesh sieve to remove all the seeds. You can also make this dish with grilled turkey tenderloin slices or grilled pork loin chops.

The raspberry sauce can be made up to 24 hours in advance and refrigerated until ready to reheat in a small saucepan.

10 ounces unsweetened thawed frozen raspberries
½ cup orange juice
2 tablespoons cornstarch
Cooking spray
2 tablespoons honey mustard
4 fully cooked ham steaks (about 3 ounces each)

In a medium saucepan, combine the raspberries, orange juice, and cornstarch. Set the pan over medium heat and bring to a simmer. Simmer for 5 to 7 minutes, until the raspberries break down and the sauce thickens.

Meanwhile, coat a stovetop grill pan or griddle with cooking spray and preheat over medium-high heat.

Brush the mustard all over both sides of the ham steaks. Add the ham to the hot pan and cook for 1 to 2 minutes per side, until browned.

Arrange the ham on a serving platter and drizzle the raspberry sauce over the top.

Cowboy Pizza with Rattlesnake Beans, Bacon & Manchego

Serves 4 ■ Prep time: 10 minutes ■ Cooking time: 15 to 20 minutes

Nutrients per serving:
Calories: 432
Fat: 8g
Saturated Fat: 4g
Cholesterol: 14mg
Carbohydrate: 68g
Protein: 20g
Fiber: 10g
Sodium: 888mg

I call this "cowboy" pizza because it boasts many of the wonderful flavors of the Southwest. Rattlesnake beans are actually hybrids of the pinto bean, and they're named after the snake because the bean pods curl and look like coiled snakes when they grow. Rattlesnake beans can be eaten fresh, like green beans, and they are often sold dried, as legumes. Since all dried beans require soaking in water and long cooking times, I used canned pinto beans on this pizza! Instead of plain pinto beans, you may substitute a can of Mexican-style beans flavored with chorizo, cilantro, and jalapeño.

As for my cheese selection, manchego is a firm sheep's milk cheese with a distinctive flavor and buttery texture. Substitute Colby or mild cheddar for the manchego, if desired. Finicky eaters might prefer the pizza without the jalapeños so you can leave them off one half of the pizza. To reduce the amount of sodium in the pizza, opt for reduced-sodium cheese and fresh jalapeños. For larger groups, simply double or triple the recipe and make multiple pizzas.

1 (14-ounce) can refrigerated pizza dough
1 (15-ounce) can pinto beans, rinsed and drained
2 slices center-cut bacon, cooked until crisp and crumbled
1 cup shredded manchego cheese
2 tablespoons minced jarred jalapeños

Preheat the oven to 400°F.

Unroll the dough onto a baking sheet and press into a 12 by 8-inch rectangle. Arrange the beans all over the dough, to within ¼ inch of the edges. Top the beans with the bacon, cheese, and jalapeños.

Bake for 15 to 20 minutes, until the crust is golden brown and the cheese is bubbly.

Spinach Salad with Blueberries, Blue Cheese & Walnuts

Serves 4 ■ Prep time: 15 minutes

Nutrients per serving:
Calories: 167
Fat: 12g
Saturated Fat: 3g
Cholesterol: 8mg
Carbohydrate: 13g
Protein: 5g
Fiber: 3g
Sodium: 195mg

Take advantage of blueberry season with this colorful and flavorful salad. Got a non-blueberry-eater in the family? Substitute raspberries, strawberries, or peaches so that you can still enjoy the sweetness that fruit adds to this salad. For more protein, add 8 ounces grilled chicken, steak, or tofu. For a wilted spinach salad, assemble the dish up to 24 hours in advance and refrigerate until ready to serve (add the walnuts just before serving so they stay crunchy). For larger groups, simply double or triple the recipe.

⅓ **cup walnut pieces**

4 **cups baby spinach**

8 **ounces fresh blueberries**

⅓ **cup crumbled blue cheese**

Juice and zest of 1 lemon

1 **tablespoon olive oil**

Salt and freshly ground black pepper

Place the walnuts in a small dry skillet over medium heat. Cook the walnuts for 3 minutes, shaking the pan frequently, until golden brown and toasted. Remove the walnuts from the heat.

In a large bowl, combine the spinach, blueberries, blue cheese, 1 tablespoon of the lemon juice, 1 teaspoon of the lemon zest, and the oil. Toss to coat the spinach with the lemon juice and oil. Season to taste with salt and pepper.

Transfer the spinach mixture to a serving platter and sprinkle the toasted walnuts over the top.

White Pizza with Pesto & Asparagus

Serves 4 ■ Prep time: 10 minutes ■ Cooking time: 15 to 20 minutes

Nutrients per serving:
Calories: 426
Fat: 16g
Saturated Fat: 6g
Cholesterol: 21mg
Carbohydrate: 51g
Protein: 21g
Fiber: 5g
Sodium: 785mg

Create finicky friendly pizzas of all types by using your family's favorite vegetables and cheeses. I like to use fresh asparagus for this dish, but you may substitute thawed frozen asparagus. When using fresh asparagus, the thinner the stalks the better, so be selective when shopping. Just don't use the jarred or canned variety, as the stalks are too mushy for pizza. For parties, add crowd-pleasing vegetables such as bell peppers, spinach, and olives. For larger groups, simply double or triple the recipe and make multiple pizzas. I used reduced-sodium cheese on this pizza to cut back on some of the salt (pesto, Parmesan, and prepared pizza dough contribute a decent amount). You can use regular part-skim mozzarella cheese if you prefer.

The pizza can be assembled up to 24 hours in advance and refrigerated until ready to bake.

1 (14-ounce) can refrigerated pizza dough

¼ cup prepared basil pesto

1 bunch asparagus, stem ends trimmed and spears cut into 2-inch pieces

1 cup shredded reduced-sodium part-skim mozzarella cheese

1 tablespoon grated Parmesan cheese

Preheat the oven to 400°F.

Unroll the dough onto a baking sheet and press into a 12 by 8-inch rectangle. Spread the pesto all over the dough, to within ¼ inch of the edges. Arrange the asparagus pieces on top of the pesto. Top with the mozzarella and Parmesan cheeses.

Bake for 15 to 20 minutes, until the crust is golden brown and the cheese is bubbly.

Eggplant Napoleons with Smoked Mozzarella & Tomato

Serves 4 ■ Prep time: 15 to 20 minutes ■ Cooking time: 10 to 15 minutes

This is a great dish to create with your kids—they can help layer the cheese and tomatoes on the grilled eggplant slices before they go into the oven. For finicky eaters, make mini napoleons with zucchini, yellow summer squash, or portobello mushroom caps instead of the eggplant.

The eggplant napoleons can be assembled up to 24 hours in advance and refrigerated until ready to bake.

Nutrients per serving:
Calories: 180
Fat: 9g
Saturated Fat: 5g
Cholesterol: 21mg
Carbohydrate: 17g
Protein: 11g
Fiber: 10g
Sodium: 277mg

> **Cooking spray**
> **2 large or 3 medium eggplant, cut crosswise into 12 slices (each about ¼ inch thick)**
> **Salt and freshly ground black pepper**
> **1 cup shredded smoked mozzarella cheese**
> **1 cup thinly sliced tomato (beefsteak or plum)**
> **4 teaspoons grated Parmesan cheese**

Preheat the oven to 350°F. Coat a shallow baking dish with cooking spray. Coat a stovetop grill pan or griddle with cooking spray and preheat over medium-high heat.

Season both sides of the eggplant slices with salt and pepper. Add the eggplant slices to the hot pan and cook for 2 to 3 minutes per side, until golden brown and tender.

Arrange one-third of the eggplant slices in the bottom of the prepared baking dish. Top the eggplant slices with half of the mozzarella and half of the tomato slices. Arrange another one-third of the eggplant slices on top of the cheese and tomato slices. Top with the remaining mozzarella cheese and the remaining tomato slices. Place the remaining eggplant slices on top and sprinkle the Parmesan over the entire surface.

Bake for 10 to 15 minutes, until the top is golden brown and the cheese melts.

Spaghetti Squash with Pesto

Serves 4 ■ Prep time: 10 to 15 minutes

Kids love how spaghetti squash resembles real spaghetti but has a little crunch to it. This dish is unbelievably crammed with flavor thanks to the fire-roasted tomatoes, pesto, pine nuts, and Parmesan cheese. It's also an excellent gluten-free option for the pasta lovers in the crowd.

The squash can be made up to 24 hours in advance and refrigerated until ready to reheat in a large saucepan over medium-low heat (if necessary, add a little water to keep the mixture moist).

1 spaghetti squash, about 2 pounds, halved lengthwise
2 tablespoons pine nuts
1 (14-ounce) can diced fire-roasted tomatoes, drained
½ cup prepared basil pesto
Salt and freshly ground black pepper
2 tablespoons grated Parmesan cheese

Nutrients per serving:
Calories: 251
Fat: 18g
Saturated Fat: 3g
Cholesterol: 12mg
Carbohydrate: 18g
Protein: 7g
Fiber: 4g
Sodium: 526mg

Place the spaghetti squash, cut side down, in a microwave-safe baking dish. Add about 1 inch of water to the dish. Cover with a paper towel and microwave on HIGH power for 5 to 7 minutes, until the flesh is tender and you can create spaghetti strands by pulling the squash with a fork (turn the dish every 2 minutes if your microwave doesn't have a spinning plate).

Meanwhile, place the pine nuts in a small dry skillet over medium heat. Cook for 3 minutes, shaking the pan frequently, until the nuts are golden brown and toasted.

Scoop the flesh from the spaghetti squash and transfer it to a large bowl. Add the tomatoes and pesto and mix well to coat the squash with the pesto. Season to taste with salt and pepper.

Arrange the squash on a serving platter and top with the Parmesan and toasted pine nuts.

Roasted Acorn Squash with Spinach & Hazelnuts

Serves 4 ■ Prep time: 10 minutes ■ Cooking time: 1 hour

Nutrients per serving:
Calories: 241
Fat: 13g
Saturated Fat: 1.5g
Cholesterol: 0mg
Carbohydrate: 33g
Protein: 5g
Fiber: 8g
Sodium: 120mg

Kids love this sweet acorn squash dish because it includes crunchy hazelnuts. For finicky eaters, you can eliminate the garlic and onion. When working with winter squash, use a sturdy chef's knife to cut the squash lengthwise from stem to end. Use a heavy spoon to scrape out the seeds. This dish also works really well with butternut squash.

- **2 medium acorn squash, halved lengthwise**
- **6 teaspoons olive oil**
- **Salt and freshly ground black pepper**
- **2 cloves garlic, minced**
- **10 ounces baby spinach**
- **2 teaspoons dried minced onion**
- **⅓ cup chopped hazelnuts**

Preheat the oven to 400°F.

Scoop out the seeds and stringy stuff from each squash half. Using a sharp knife, score the inside of each squash half several times. Place the halves in a shallow baking dish, cut side up. Add about ¼ inch of water to the bottom of the baking dish to prevent the skins from burning. Brush the inside of each squash half with 1 teaspoon of the olive oil and season to taste with salt and pepper.

Bake for 1 hour, until the squash is very soft and the tops are browned.

Meanwhile, heat the remaining 2 teaspoons oil in a large skillet over medium-high heat. Add the garlic and cook for 1 minute. Add the spinach and onion and cook for 2 minutes, or until the spinach wilts. Season to taste with salt and pepper.

Arrange the squash halves on a serving platter. Fill each squash half with spinach and top with the hazelnuts.

Roasted Tomato, Basil & Provolone Panini

Serves 4 ■ Prep time: 35 minutes ■ Cooking time: 10 minutes

Roasting tomatoes helps remove some of their liquid while adding a layer of sweet flavor. That sweetness is perfectly contrasted with the balsamic glaze, basil, and nutty provolone in this recipe. Make extra panini because the leftovers are a great addition to the lunch box for work and school. For larger groups, simply double or triple the recipe. If you don't have a panini press, cook the sandwiches in a large skillet, pressing them down with a heavy pan while cooking.

The tomatoes can be roasted up to 24 hours in advance and refrigerated until ready to assemble the sandwiches.

Nutrients per serving:
Calories: 294
Fat: 16g
Saturated Fat: 10g
Cholesterol: 39mg
Carbohydrate: 21g
Protein: 17g
Fiber: 2g
Sodium: 622mg

Cooking spray
2 large beefsteak tomatoes or 4 plum tomatoes, sliced crosswise into ½-inch-thick slices
Salt and freshly ground black pepper
8 teaspoons balsamic glaze or syrup
8 slices Italian bread (about ½ inch thick) or 4 sub rolls
8 slices provolone cheese (about 8 ounces total)
½ cup fresh basil leaves

Preheat the oven to 350°F. Coat a large baking sheet with cooking spray.

Arrange the tomato slices on the prepared baking sheet and season to taste with salt and pepper. Roast for 30 minutes, or until the tomatoes are shriveled and golden brown.

Coat a panini press or large skillet with cooking spray and preheat to medium-high.

Spread the balsamic glaze on the slices of bread or inside the sub rolls. Top 4 of the bread slices with the tomatoes, cheese, and basil. Place the second slice of bread on top, glaze side in (or close the rolls), and transfer the sandwiches to the panini press. Cook the sandwiches according to the manufacturer's instructions (if using a skillet, press the sandwiches down with a heavy pan and cook for 3 to 4 minutes per side, until the bread is golden brown and the cheese melts). Serve warm or at room temperature.

CHICKEN

Havana Black Bean Chili with Chicken

Braised Chicken with Pomegranate Glaze

Sweet-and-Sour Chicken with Mixed Dried Fruit

Chicken with Balsamic-Glazed Onions & Bell Peppers

Italian Chicken with Baby Carrots

Jerk Turkey Tenderloin with Pineapple

BEEF

Beef Roast with Black Bean Sauce & Baby Corn

Pot Roast Pomodoro with Shaved Parmesan

Sweet-and-Sour Beef Brisket

Moroccan Braised Beef Brisket

Beef Brisket with Green Pepper Jelly Barbecue Sauce

Braised Short Ribs with Roasted Red Pepper Sauce

PORK

Carolina Pulled Pork

Ham & Swiss–Stuffed Pork Loin with Applesauce

Pork Roast with Cinnamon Pears & Fingerling Potatoes

Mexican Pork

Root Beer–Braised Ribs

Pork Carnitas

CHAPTER 5

Start Slow, Finish Fast: Slow Cooker Meals

Havana Black Bean Chili with Chicken

Serves 4 ■ Prep time: 10 minutes ■ Cooking time: 6 to 8 hours

I love to serve this warm dish for parties because it's a breeze to prepare and I can serve it in hollowed rolls or bread bowls. You can also serve the chili over rice. For larger groups, simply double or triple the recipe and feel free to add a variety of vegetables, such as carrots, celery, bell peppers, zucchini, and/or corn. Add the vegetables when you add the black beans. For a little heat, add a seeded and minced jalapeño pepper. For added flavor at the end, add 2 tablespoons chopped fresh cilantro just before serving.

Nutrients per serving:
Calories: 430
Fat: 4g
Saturated Fat: 1g
Cholesterol: 72mg
Carbohydrate: 55g
Protein: 43g
Fiber: 18g
Sodium: 822mg

1 pound boneless, skinless chicken breasts, cut into 1-inch pieces

2 (14-ounce) cans diced tomatoes with green pepper, celery, and onion, undrained

1 tablespoon chili powder

1 teaspoon ground cumin

2 (15-ounce) cans black beans, rinsed and drained

In the bottom of a slow cooker, combine the chicken, tomatoes, chili powder, and cumin. Mix well. Cover and cook on low for 6 to 8 hours.

Stir in the black beans, cover, and cook for 5 minutes, or until the beans are hot.

Braised Chicken with Pomegranate Glaze

Serves 4 ■ Prep time: 10 minutes ■ Cooking time: 6 to 8 hours

Plum sauce is a sweet-and-sour condiment used in Asian cooking. Your whole family will love how it partners with tart pomegranate juice. For a great presentation, top the chicken with pomegranate seeds just before serving.

4 bone-in, skinless chicken breast halves (about 7 ounces each)
Salt and freshly ground black pepper
1 cup plum sauce
⅓ cup pomegranate juice
1 tablespoon reduced-sodium soy sauce
¼ cup chopped scallions (white and green parts)

Season both sides of the chicken with salt and pepper. Arrange the chicken in the bottom of a slow cooker.

In a medium bowl, combine the plum sauce, pomegranate juice, soy sauce, and scallions. Mix well and pour the mixture over the chicken.

Cover and cook on low for 6 to 8 hours, until the chicken is cooked through.

Nutrients per serving:
Calories: 297
Fat: 4g
Saturated Fat: 1g
Cholesterol: 72mg
Carbohydrate: 36g
Protein: 28g
Fiber: 1g
Sodium: 574mg

Sweet-and-Sour Chicken with Mixed Dried Fruit

Serves 4 ■ Prep time: 10 minutes ■ Cooking time: 6 to 8 hours

Kids love the sweetness that dried fruit and apple cider add to this dish. It's the perfect dish for fall birthday celebrations and other parties. For larger groups, simply double the recipe. For variety, you can use a 1-pound pork loin roast instead of the chicken.

Nutrients per serving:
Calories: 320
Fat: 3g
Saturated Fat: 1g
Cholesterol: 72mg
Carbohydrate: 44g
Protein: 28g
Fiber: 5g
Sodium: 156mg

½ cup sliced red onion

4 bone-in, skinless chicken breast halves (about 7 ounces each)

Salt and freshly ground black pepper

1 (8-ounce) package mixed dried fruit pieces (such as apricots, apples, pears, and plums) (1½ cups)

1 cup apple cider

1 teaspoon ground cumin

Arrange the onion in the bottom of a slow cooker. Season both sides of the chicken with salt and pepper and place on top of the onion. Place the dried fruit on top of the chicken. Whisk together the cider and cumin and pour the mixture over the chicken and dried fruit.

Cover and cook on low for 6 to 8 hours, until the chicken is cooked through.

Chicken with Balsamic-Glazed Onions & Bell Peppers

Serves 4 ■ Prep time: 10 minutes ■ Cooking time: 6 to 8 hours

If you have kids who claim they don't like onions, experiment with small pearl onions. They're sweeter than other onions and add great flavor to a variety of dishes. In this meal, they're especially sweet after simmering in the balsamic glaze. I also add red and green bell peppers, but you may use a variety of fresh (or frozen) vegetables instead.

Nutrients per serving:
Calories: 257
Fat: 3g
Saturated Fat: 1g
Cholesterol: 72mg
Carbohydrate: 27g
Protein: 27g
Fiber: 2g
Sodium: 106mg

1 (16-ounce) package frozen pearl onions
⅓ cup plus 2 tablespoons balsamic glaze or syrup
4 bone-in, skinless chicken breast halves (about 7 ounces each)
Salt and freshly ground black pepper
2 bell peppers (preferably 1 red and 1 green), seeded and cut into thin strips
2 tablespoons chopped fresh parsley

In a large bowl, combine the onions and ⅓ cup of the balsamic glaze. Stir to coat the onions with the glaze. Arrange the onions in the bottom of a slow cooker.

Season both sides of the chicken with salt and pepper and place on top of the onions.

In a medium bowl, combine the bell peppers and the remaining 2 tablespoons balsamic glaze. Stir to coat the peppers with the glaze. Arrange the peppers on top of the chicken.

Cover and cook on low for 6 to 8 hours, until the chicken is cooked through.

Transfer the chicken and vegetables to a serving platter and sprinkle the parsley over the top.

Italian Chicken with Baby Carrots

Serves 4 ■ Prep time: 10 minutes ■ Cooking time: 6 to 8 hours

Nutrients per serving:
Calories: 193
Fat: 3g
Saturated Fat: 1g
Cholesterol: 72mg
Carbohydrate: 11g
Protein: 29g
Fiber: 2g
Sodium: 113mg

The chicken in this dish gets its flavor not only from the coating of Italian seasoning but also by cooking on top of the sliced onion while simmering in good-quality broth (sometimes I use roasted garlic chicken broth). The best part about the meal is that you can add any vegetables you like. Fresh or frozen corn or peas, fingerling potatoes, zucchini, broccoli florets, and/or green beans make great additions. Add the vegetables to the slow cooker 1 hour before you plan to serve and eat.

1 cup chopped yellow onion

4 bone-in, skinless chicken breast halves (about 7 ounces each)

Salt and freshly ground black pepper

2 teaspoons salt-free Italian seasoning

2 cups baby carrots

1 cup reduced-sodium chicken broth

Arrange the onion in the bottom of a slow cooker. Season both sides of the chicken with salt and pepper and place on top of the onion. Rub the Italian seasoning into the top of the chicken. Arrange the carrots alongside the chicken and pour the broth over the chicken and carrots.

Cover and cook on low for 6 to 8 hours, until the chicken is cooked through.

Jerk Turkey Tenderloin with Pineapple

Serves 4 ■ Prep time: 10 minutes ■ Cooking time: 6 to 8 hours

Jerk seasoning is an incredible blend of herbs and spices, namely allspice, cloves, nutmeg, chile peppers, garlic, and other bold spices. Since many store-bought jerk seasonings also contain a decent amount of salt, I didn't season the turkey with salt before coating it with the seasoning. If you find a salt-free brand, season the turkey with salt and freshly ground black pepper before adding the seasoning. And, for an authentic Jamaican treat, garnish the dish with lime wedges—fresh lime juice brings out the jerk flavor to its full potential. For larger groups, simply double the recipe.

Nutrients per serving:
Calories: 195
Fat: 2g
Saturated Fat: 0g
Cholesterol: 34mg
Carbohydrate: 22g
Protein: 24g
Fiber: 1g
Sodium: 212mg

1 (8-ounce) can sliced pineapple rounds in 100% juice, drained
2 Yukon gold potatoes, thinly sliced (peeled, if desired)
2 teaspoons jerk seasoning
1 (1-pound) turkey tenderloin
1 cup reduced-sodium chicken broth

Arrange the pineapple in the bottom of a slow cooker. Arrange the potato slices over the pineapple.

Rub the jerk seasoning all over the turkey tenderloin and arrange the turkey on top of the pineapple and potatoes. Pour the broth over and around the turkey (just drizzle a little over the top so you don't wash off the jerk seasoning).

Cover and cook on low for 6 to 8 hours, until the turkey is cooked through.

Slice the turkey crosswise into 1-inch-thick slices and serve with the potatoes and pineapple.

Beef Roast with Black Bean Sauce & Baby Corn

Serves 4 ■ Prep time: 10 minutes ■ Cooking time: 8 to 10 hours

Nutrients per serving:
Calories: 374
Fat: 16g
Saturated Fat: 4g
Cholesterol: 98mg
Carbohydrate: 23g
Protein: 35g
Fiber: 3g
Sodium: 714mg

Black bean sauce is a soy-based sauce made with fermented black beans. It adds incredible depth to the meat in this dish, making it an ideal meal for diners of all ages. Look for black bean sauce with the other Asian ingredients in the grocery store. For larger groups, simply double the recipe.

1 tablespoon canola oil

1½ pounds beef round roast

Salt and freshly ground black pepper

2 stalks celery, chopped

4 scallions, chopped (white and green parts)

1 (14-ounce) can baby corn, drained

1 cup black bean sauce

Heat the oil in a large skillet over medium-high heat. Season the roast all over with salt and pepper and add to the hot pan. Cook for 5 minutes, turning frequently, until the roast is browned on all sides. Remove from the heat.

Arrange the celery and scallions in the bottom of a slow cooker. Arrange the roast on top of the vegetables. Arrange the corn alongside the roast. Pour the black bean sauce all over the roast.

Cover and cook on low for 8 to 10 hours, until the beef is tender.

Pot Roast Pomodoro with Shaved Parmesan

Serves 4 ■ Prep time: 10 minutes ■ Cooking time: 8 to 10 hours

Everyone will love this combination of tender beef, tomatoes, and Parmesan cheese. Plus, slow cooker meals make great birthday party fare because you can prep everything in advance and let the slow cooker do the work while you get ready for the festivities. The best part? Your house will smell amazing when the guests arrive. For larger groups, simply double or triple the recipe.

Nutrients per serving:
Calories: 334
Fat: 18g
Saturated Fat: 5g
Cholesterol: 72mg
Carbohydrate: 8g
Protein: 33g
Fiber: 2g
Sodium: 412mg

1 tablespoon olive oil

1½ pounds boneless beef chuck roast

Salt and freshly ground black pepper

1 tablespoon salt-free Italian seasoning

1 (14-ounce) can fire-roasted diced tomatoes, undrained

½ cup chopped oil-packed sun-dried tomatoes

¼ cup shaved Parmesan cheese

Heat the oil in a large skillet over medium-high heat. Season the roast all over with salt and pepper and add to the hot pan. Cook for 5 minutes, turning frequently, until the roast is browned on all sides. Remove from the heat.

Arrange the roast in the bottom of a slow cooker. Rub the Italian seasoning into the top and sides of the roast. Spread the diced and sun-dried tomatoes over the roast. Cover and cook on low for 8 to 10 hours, until the beef is tender.

Slice the beef and arrange on a serving platter. Top the beef with the tomatoes from the slow cooker. Top with the shaved Parmesan.

Sweet-and-Sour Beef Brisket

Serves 4 ■ Prep time: 10 minutes ■ Cooking time: 8 to 10 hours

The sweet cranberries pair wonderfully with the tender beef in this dish, so consider it for your next birthday party, potluck dinner, or block party. For larger groups, simply double or triple the amount of beef and double the amount of the other ingredients. When I make the meal for larger crowds, I like to serve the brisket and sauce on a large serving platter with small rolls on the side.

½ cup thinly sliced red onion

1½ pounds beef brisket

Salt and freshly ground black pepper

1 (16-ounce) can whole berry cranberry sauce

1 (8-ounce) can tomato sauce

1 tablespoon Dijon mustard

Nutrients per serving:
Calories: 363
Fat: 9g
Saturated Fat: 3g
Cholesterol: 70mg
Carbohydrate: 48g
Protein: 25g
Fiber: 3g
Sodium: 502mg

Arrange the onion in the bottom of a slow cooker. Season the beef all over with salt and pepper and place on top of the onion.

In a medium bowl, combine the cranberry sauce, tomato sauce, and mustard and mix well. Pour the mixture over the beef.

Cover and cook on low for 8 to 10 hours, until the beef is tender.

Cut the beef across the grain into thin slices and serve with the cranberry mixture spooned over the top.

Moroccan Braised Beef Brisket

Serves 4 ■ Prep time: 10 minutes ■ Cooking time: 8 to 10 hours

You might not consider a dish with curry to be finicky friendly, but the sometimes assertive flavor of curry paste is tamed here by the sweet apricot preserves. Curry paste is available in mild and hot versions, so select the variety that works for your family. For added color and flavor, garnish the finished dish with 2 tablespoons chopped fresh cilantro. For larger groups, simply double or triple the amount of beef and double the amount of the other ingredients.

Nutrients per serving:
Calories: 412
Fat: 10g
Saturated Fat: 3g
Cholesterol: 70mg
Carbohydrate: 58g
Protein: 24g
Fiber: 1g
Sodium: 152mg

2 large red potatoes, thinly sliced
1½ pounds beef brisket
Salt and freshly ground black pepper
1 cup apricot preserves
1 tablespoon Thai or Indian curry paste of your choice
1 teaspoon ground cumin

Arrange the potato slices in the bottom of a slow cooker. Season the beef all over with salt and pepper and place on top of the potato slices.

In a medium bowl, combine the apricot preserves, curry paste, and cumin. Mix well and spread the mixture over the beef.

Cover and cook on low for 8 to 10 hours, until the beef is tender.

Cut the beef across the grain into thin slices and serve with the potatoes on the side and apricot mixture spooned over the top.

Beef Brisket with Green Pepper Jelly Barbecue Sauce

Serves 4 ■ Prep time: 10 minutes ■ Cooking time: 8 to 10 hours

This makes a great dish for parties because you can quickly and easily catapult store-bought barbecue sauce to a new level by adding green pepper jelly. The sweet-savory jelly adds great flavor but no heat.

You can also serve the sliced brisket on soft rolls for a handheld feast. For larger groups, simply double or triple the amount of beef and double the amount of the other ingredients.

- **1 green bell pepper, seeded and thinly sliced**
- **2 stalks celery, chopped**
- **1½ pounds beef brisket**
- **Salt and freshly ground black pepper**
- **1 cup reduced-sodium barbecue sauce of your choice**
- **½ cup green pepper jelly**

Arrange the bell pepper and celery in the bottom of a slow cooker. Season the beef all over with salt and pepper and place on top of the bell pepper and celery.

In a medium bowl, combine the barbecue sauce and green pepper jelly. Mix well and spread the mixture over the beef.

Cover and cook on low for 8 to 10 hours, until the beef is tender.

Cut the beef across the grain into thin slices and serve with the sauce spooned over the top.

Braised Short Ribs with Roasted Red Pepper Sauce

Serves 4 ■ Prep time: 10 to 15 minutes ■ Cooking time: 9 to 10 hours

Nutrients per serving:
Calories: 231
Fat: 12g
Saturated Fat: 5g
Cholesterol: 67mg
Carbohydrate: 6g
Protein: 23g
Fiber: 1g
Sodium: 388mg

I like to cook these ribs in two stages. The first stage cooks the ribs to perfection in 8 to 9 hours. Then, the cooking liquid (basically water and fat) is drained away before the ribs cook for an additional hour in my smoky roasted red pepper sauce. This also makes a great dish for parties because all the work will be finished before the guests arrive. For larger groups, simply double or triple the amount of ribs and double the amount of the other ingredients.

The red pepper sauce can be prepared up to 24 hours in advance and refrigerated until ready to pour over the ribs.

Cooking spray
2 pounds short ribs
Salt and freshly ground black pepper
2 teaspoons salt-free all-purpose seasoning or Italian seasoning
1½ cups chopped roasted red peppers
2 tablespoons sun-dried tomato paste
1 teaspoon liquid smoke

Spray the bottom of a slow cooker with cooking spray.

Season the ribs all over with salt and pepper. Rub the all-purpose seasoning onto both sides of the ribs. Cut the ribs into 2- or 3-rib portions and place them in the bottom of the slow cooker. Pour over ½ cup of water.

Cover and cook on low for 8 to 9 hours, until the ribs are tender.

Meanwhile, in a blender, combine the red peppers, tomato paste, and liquid smoke. Puree until smooth.

Remove the ribs from the slow cooker and drain away the liquid from the cooker. Return the ribs to the slow cooker and pour the red pepper sauce over the top. Cover and cook on low for 1 more hour.

Carolina Pulled Pork

Serves 4 ■ Prep time: 10 minutes ■ Cooking time: 8 to 10 hours

This mouthwatering pork is tender and juicy and boasts the distinct flavors of apple cider, Dijon mustard, Worcestershire sauce, and smoked paprika. It's excellent when served on soft rolls.

Store leftover shredded pork in the refrigerator for up to 3 days. Reheat in a saucepan over low heat or in the microwave. For larger groups, simply double or triple the amount of pork and double the amount of the other ingredients.

1 (1-pound) boneless pork loin roast
Salt and freshly ground black pepper
1 cup apple cider
1 tablespoon Dijon mustard
1 teaspoon Worcestershire sauce
1 teaspoon smoked paprika

Nutrients per serving:
Calories: 160
Fat: 5g
Saturated Fat: 2g
Cholesterol: 54mg
Carbohydrate: 9g
Protein: 18g
Fiber: <1g
Sodium: 153mg

Season the pork all over with salt and pepper and place in the bottom of a slow cooker.

Whisk together the apple cider, mustard, Worcestershire sauce, and smoked paprika and pour the sauce over the pork.

Cover and cook on low for 8 to 10 hours, until the pork is very tender.

Transfer the pork to a serving platter and, using two forks, pull it apart into shreds. Spoon over any remaining sauce from the slow cooker.

Ham & Swiss–Stuffed Pork Loin with Applesauce

Serves 4 ■ Prep time: 10 to 15 minutes ■ Cooking time: 8 to 10 hours

Nutrients per serving:
Calories: 296
Fat: 15g
Saturated Fat: 7g
Cholesterol: 89mg
Carbohydrate: 10g
Protein: 30g
Fiber: 1g
Sodium: 518mg

There are few things in life better than ham-and-cheese-stuffed pork loin with applesauce. Except maybe when the applesauce is spiked with sweet and tangy honey mustard. This undeniably dynamite blend of flavors will please even the finickiest palates. For larger groups, simply double or triple the amount of pork and double the amount of the other ingredients.

1 (1-pound) boneless pork loin roast
4 ounces smoked ham, thinly sliced
4 ounces Swiss cheese, thinly sliced
Salt and freshly ground black pepper
⅔ cup unsweetened applesauce
2 tablespoons honey mustard

Using a sharp knife, cut a pocket into the center of the pork roast, leaving about ½ inch around the edges intact. Stuff the ham and Swiss into the pocket. Season the pork all over with salt and pepper and place in the bottom of a slow cooker, cut side up.

In a small bowl, whisk together the applesauce and honey mustard. Pour the mixture over the pork.

Cover and cook on low for 8 to 10 hours, until the pork is very tender.

Slice the pork crosswise to reveal the filling and serve with the applesauce mixture spooned over the top.

Pork Roast with Cinnamon Pears & Fingerling Potatoes

Serves 4 ■ Prep time: 10 minutes ■ Cooking time: 8 to 10 hours

Ever since I discovered canned pears spiked with cinnamon, I've been finding savory applications for the sweet, warming fruit. It partners incredibly well with the pork, red onion, and Dijon mustard in this meal. Kids love the look and taste of little fingerling potatoes. If you can find them, use a medley of red, gold, and purple fingerling potatoes; they add great color to the feast. For finicky eaters, eliminate the onion, replacing it with baby carrots, if desired.

Nutrients per serving:
Calories: 241
Fat: 6g
Saturated Fat: 2g
Cholesterol: 54mg
Carbohydrate: 28g
Protein: 19g
Fiber: 5g
Sodium: 142mg

½ cup thinly sliced red onion

2 cups small fingerling potatoes

1 (1-pound) boneless pork loin roast

Salt and freshly ground black pepper

1 (15-ounce) can cinnamon-flavored pear halves, drained and liquid reserved

1 tablespoon Dijon mustard

Arrange the onion and potatoes in the bottom of a slow cooker. Season the pork all over with salt and pepper and place on top of the onion and potatoes.

In a small bowl, whisk together the liquid from the canned pears and the mustard. Pour the mixture over the pork. Arrange the pear halves over the pork.

Cover and cook on low for 8 to 10 hours, until the pork is very tender.

Slice the pork and serve with the pear halves, potatoes, and onion.

Mexican Pork

Serves 4 ■ Prep time: 10 minutes ■ Cooking time: 6 to 8 hours

This is a terrific combination of Mexican flavors: salsa, green chiles, beans, and cheese. For finicky eaters, you can replace the pork with boneless, skinless chicken breasts or turkey tenderloin (also cut into 1-inch pieces). For parties, serve soft flour tortillas, shredded lettuce, and guacamole on the side so folks can create handheld soft tacos. For larger groups, simply double or triple the recipe.

1 (1-pound) boneless pork loin roast, cut into 1-inch pieces
2½ cups salsa of your choice
1 (4-ounce) can chopped green chiles
1 (15-ounce) can black beans, rinsed and drained
1 cup shredded Monterey Jack cheese

Nutrients per serving:
Calories: 409
Fat: 15g
Saturated Fat: 7g
Cholesterol: 80mg
Carbohydrate: 34g
Protein: 35g
Fiber: 11g
Sodium: 899mg

Combine the pork, salsa, and chiles in the bottom of a slow cooker. Cover and cook on low for 6 to 8 hours, until the pork is tender.

Stir in the black beans, cover, and cook for 5 minutes, or until the beans are hot.

Transfer the pork mixture to a serving platter and top with the Monterey Jack cheese.

Root Beer–Braised Ribs

Serves 4 ■ Prep time: 10 to 15 minutes ■ Cooking time: 9 to 10 hours

Kids love root beer, and there's no better way to braise ribs than with a glaze of root beer, barbecue sauce, and sun-dried tomato paste. Because you cook the ribs in two stages (stage one cooks them completely and eliminates excess fat, and stage two infuses the flavor of the root beer glaze), the dish is excellent for parties. The preparation is practically complete before the doorbell rings. Plus, ribs are true crowd-pleasers. For larger groups, simply double or triple the amount of ribs and double the amount of the other ingredients.

Nutrients per serving:
Calories: 341
Fat: 19g
Saturated Fat: 7g
Cholesterol: 78mg
Carbohydrate: 20g
Protein: 21g
Fiber: 1g
Sodium: 465mg

Cooking spray
2 pounds pork loin back ribs or pork spareribs
Salt and freshly ground black pepper
1 cup root beer
½ cup barbecue sauce of your choice
2 tablespoons sun-dried tomato paste

Spray the bottom of a slow cooker with cooking spray. Season the ribs all over with salt and pepper. Cut the ribs into 2- or 3-rib portions and place them in the bottom of the slow cooker. Pour over ½ cup of water.

Cover and cook on low for 8 to 9 hours, until the ribs are tender.

Remove the ribs from the slow cooker and drain away the liquid from the cooker. Return the ribs to the slow cooker. Whisk together the root beer, barbecue sauce, and tomato paste. Pour the mixture over the ribs. Cover and cook on low for 1 hour.

Pork Carnitas

Serves 4 ■ Prep time: 10 minutes ■ Cooking time: 8 to 10 hours

Carnitas are a Mexican dish consisting of seasoned pulled pork that's cooked until tender and then fried in lard. The result is a delightful contrast of tender pork meat with crispy brown edges. To create a similar dish at home with half the ingredients and effort, I let the slow cooker do all the tenderizing and the broiler do all the browning! The pork is fabulous in sandwiches and as a filling for tamales, tacos, enchiladas, and burritos. In this dish, I arrange the meat on warm corn tortillas so you can enjoy a handheld treat. For added flavor and color, add diced tomato, minced white onion, shredded cheddar cheese or cotija cheese, lime wedges, and fresh cilantro.

Nutrients per serving:
Calories: 397
Fat: 13g
Saturated Fat: 4g
Cholesterol: 98mg
Carbohydrate: 32g
Protein: 37g
Fiber: 4g
Sodium: 597mg

2 pounds boneless pork shoulder (or 2½ pounds bone-in)
Salt and freshly ground black pepper
1 packet taco seasoning
1 cup salsa of your choice
1 orange, halved
12 corn tortillas

Rinse the pork shoulder with water and pat dry. Season the pork all over with salt and pepper. Rub the taco seasoning all over the pork and place the pork in a slow cooker. Pour the salsa over the pork. Squeeze the juice of the orange over the pork and arrange the two halves on top of the pork. Cover and cook on low for 8 to 10 hours, until the meat is very tender.

Remove the pork from the slow cooker and, when cool enough to handle, pull the meat apart with two forks.

Preheat the broiler. Arrange the pork on a large baking sheet. Place the pork under the broiler and cook for 2 to 3 minutes, until the meat is browned and crispy on the edges. Warm the corn tortillas in the microwave on HIGH power for 20 to 30 seconds.

Serve the pork in the corn tortillas.

Parmesan Fries
Ghoulish Twice-Baked Potato "Faces"
Whipped Sweet Potatoes
Creamy Buttermilk Mashed Potatoes
Scalloped Yukon Golds with Smoked Mozzarella
Barbecue Baked Potato Chips
Grilled Portobello "Fries"
Baked Ranch Onion Rings
Jicama Sticks with Roasted Red Pepper Dip
Butternut Squash with Maple Butter
Grilled Honey-Lime Corn
Maple-Dijon Roasted Brussels Sprouts
Roasted Asparagus with Sun-Dried Tomato Bits
Braised Root Vegetables with Balsamic Glaze
Parmesan-Stuffed Pretzels with Honey Mustard
Sweet Potato Fries with Maple-Dijon Dip
Green Apple Salad with Gorgonzola & Almonds
Celery Stalk Caesar Salad
Cucumber & Fresh Dill Salad
Asian Broccoli Slaw with Toasted Sesame Seeds
Guacamole with a Sour Cream "Spiderweb" & Blue Chips
Spinach Salad with Honey-Bacon Dressing
Cranberry Chutney with Onion & Golden Raisins

CHAPTER 6

Vegetable Side Dishes *All* Kids Crave

Parmesan Fries

Serves 4 ■ Prep time: 10 minutes ■ Cooking time: 25 to 30 minutes

I like to cut these potatoes into wedges, but you can cut them into thick matchstick shapes instead. The potatoes can be peeled or left unpeeled; we like the skins on in our house. I've also made these fries with Yukon gold potatoes, so choose whatever variety you have on hand. For garlic-Parmesan fries, sprinkle the potatoes with a little garlic powder before adding the Parmesan cheese. For parties, serve the fries with Chicken Fingers with Peanut Sauce (page 98) or Grilled Chicken Strips with Orange Marmalade Ketchup (page 89). For larger groups, simply double or triple the recipe.

Nutrients per serving:
Calories: 86
Fat: <1g
Saturated Fat: <1g
Cholesterol: 1mg
Carbohydrate: 18g
Protein: 3g
Fiber: 2g
Sodium: 28mg

Cooking spray
2 large baking (russet) potatoes, cut into 8 wedges each
Salt and freshly ground black pepper
1 tablespoon grated Parmesan cheese

Preheat the oven to 400°F. Coat a large baking sheet with cooking spray.

Arrange the potato wedges on the prepared baking sheet and spray the surface of the potatoes with cooking spray. Season the potatoes with salt and pepper and then sprinkle with the Parmesan.

Bake for 25 to 30 minutes, until the potatoes are golden brown and tender.

Ghoulish Twice-Baked Potato "Faces"

Serves 4 ■ Prep time: 1 hour ■ Cooking time: 15 minutes

Nutrients per serving:
Calories: 228
Fat: 8g
Saturated Fat: 5g
Cholesterol: 25mg
Carbohydrate: 32g
Protein: 9g
Fiber: 3g
Sodium: 141g

These fun and delicious "faces" are excellent for parties and Halloween celebrations. When it comes to baking potatoes, I like the way oven cooking creates a crunchy skin, so I bake them in the oven both times. That said, to speed up prep time, you may cook the whole potatoes in the microwave for the first round of cooking. To do that, prick the potatoes with a fork and then microwave on HIGH power for 7 to 8 minutes, until fork-tender, turning every 2 minutes if your microwave doesn't have a spinning plate. Proceed as directed below from step 3.

The stuffed potatoes can be assembled up to 24 hours in advance and refrigerated until ready to bake. For larger groups, simply double or triple the recipe.

4 small baking (russet) potatoes
Cooking spray
Salt and freshly ground black pepper
½ cup light sour cream
½ cup mild or sharp shredded cheddar cheese
Sliced black olives
Sliced pimentos or roasted red peppers

Preheat the oven to 425°F.

Spray the outside of the potatoes with cooking spray and place them on a baking sheet. Cut a small slit in the top of each potato and bake for 45 minutes, or until the potatoes are soft. Remove the potatoes from the oven and decrease the oven temperature to 375°F.

When the potatoes are cool enough to handle, halve them lengthwise and scoop out the flesh to make ¼-inch-thick shells. Transfer the flesh to a medium bowl and add in the sour cream and cheddar cheese. Mix well. Spoon the mixture back into the potato skins.

Transfer the potatoes back to the baking sheet and bake for 15 minutes, or until the cheese melts and the tops are golden brown.

To make the ghoulish faces, use the black olives to make the eyes, and make a circle mouth with the pimentos or roasted red pepper slices.

Whipped Sweet Potatoes

Serves 4 ■ Prep time: 20 minutes

Everyone loves the sweetness of brown sugar coupled with sweet potatoes. For a holiday treat, you can spoon the whipped sweet potatoes into a casserole dish, top them with mini marshmallows, and bake for 15 minutes at 350°F, until the marshmallows are golden brown. And, if desired, you may substitute light sour cream for the Greek yogurt.

The whipped sweet potatoes can be made up to 24 hours in advance and refrigerated until ready to reheat in the microwave.

Nutrients per serving:
Calories: 126
Fat: <1g
Saturated Fat: 0g
Cholesterol: 2mg
Carbohydrate: 28g
Protein: 3g
Fiber: 3g
Sodium: 54g

2 large sweet potatoes, peeled and cut into 2-inch pieces
½ cup low-fat plain Greek yogurt
2 tablespoons light brown sugar
½ teaspoon ground cinnamon
Salt and freshly ground black pepper

Place the sweet potatoes in a large saucepan and pour over enough water to cover by about 2 inches. Set the pan over high heat and bring to a boil. Boil for 10 minutes, or until the potatoes are fork-tender.

Drain and return the potatoes to the pan. Add the yogurt, brown sugar, and cinnamon and, using a potato masher, mash together until blended (for a very smooth consistency, puree the mixture in a food processor). Season to taste with salt and pepper.

Creamy Buttermilk Mashed Potatoes

Serves 4 ■ Prep time: 20 minutes

Most kids adore ranch dressing, and my kids are no different. That's why these creamy, ranch-spiked spuds are a huge hit in my house. They're actually a Thanksgiving staple. The optional herbs make them super finicky friendly. If you've got onion lovers, fold in chopped scallions at the end.

The mashed potatoes can be made up to 24 hours in advance and refrigerated until ready to reheat in the microwave.

Nutrients per serving:
Calories: 213
Fat: 4g
Saturated Fat: 1g
Cholesterol: 1mg
Carbohydrate: 22g
Protein: 3g
Fiber: 2g
Sodium: 481mg

2 large (russet) potatoes, peeled and cut into 2-inch pieces
½ cup low-fat buttermilk, plus more as needed
2 tablespoons powdered ranch dressing mix
1 tablespoon olive oil
Salt and freshly ground black pepper
2 tablespoons chopped fresh chives and/or parsley (optional)

Place the potatoes in a large saucepan and pour over enough water to cover by about 2 inches. Set the pan over high heat and bring to a boil. Boil for 10 minutes, or until the potatoes are fork-tender.

Drain and return the potatoes to the pan. Add the buttermilk, ranch dressing mix, and oil. Using a potato masher, mash together until blended (for a very smooth consistency, puree the mixture in a food processor). Season to taste with salt and pepper. Fold in the herbs, if using.

Scalloped Yukon Golds with Smoked Mozzarella

Serves 4 ■ Prep time: 15 minutes ■ Cooking time: 1 hour

It's wonderful how much enormous flavor smoked cheese can add to a dish. The addition of Dijon mustard actually brings out even more cheesy goodness. I like using Yukon gold potatoes in this dish, but you can certainly use regular baking/ russet potatoes instead. For super-finicky eaters, decide if you should use regular mozzarella cheese or the smoked variety.

The scalloped potatoes can be assembled up to 24 hours in advance and refrigerated until ready to bake. For larger groups, simply double or triple the recipe and bake the potatoes in two to three different baking dishes.

Cooking spray
4 medium Yukon gold potatoes, sliced ¼ inch thick
2 cups shredded smoked mozzarella cheese
Freshly ground black pepper
1 cup low-fat (1%) milk
1 teaspoon Dijon mustard

Preheat the oven to 375°F. Coat a shallow baking dish (about 11 by 7 inches) with cooking spray.

Arrange one-quarter of the potato slices in the bottom of the prepared baking dish, allowing the slices to overlap slightly. Top the potatoes with ½ cup of the cheese and pepper to taste. Repeat the layering, creating four layers of potatoes and four layers of cheese.

Whisk together the milk and mustard and drizzle the mixture over the potatoes and cheese. Press down the potatoes with a fork to allow the milk to coat everything.

Bake for 1 hour, until the potatoes are tender and the cheese is golden brown and bubbly.

Barbecue Baked Potato Chips

Serves 4 ■ Prep time: 10 minutes ■ Cooking time: 20 to 25 minutes

Adults and kids alike love barbecue-flavored potato chips, so there's no question the whole family will love my baked version. The flavoring in my baked chips comes from mesquite seasoning, a wonderful, smoky spice that's sold with the other seasonings in the spice aisle (near the grilling spices). You can also make these chips with regular baking/russet potatoes; peel them or not, as you prefer (we like to leave the skins on). One tip: The thinner you slice the potatoes, the crispier they will become when they bake. For larger groups, simply double or triple the recipe.

Nutrients per serving:
Calories: 140
Fat: 0g
Saturated Fat: 0g
Cholesterol: 0mg
Carbohydrate: 30g
Protein: 4g
Fiber: 2g
Sodium: 150mg

Cooking spray
4 medium Yukon gold potatoes, sliced ⅛ inch thick
2 teaspoons mesquite seasoning

Preheat the oven to 375°F. Coat a large baking sheet with cooking spray.

Arrange the potato slices on the prepared baking sheet. Spray the potato slices with cooking spray and sprinkle with the mesquite seasoning.

Bake for 20 to 25 minutes, until the potatoes are golden brown and crisp.

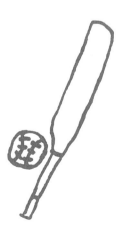

Grilled Portobello "Fries"

Serves 4 ■ Prep time: 10 minutes ■ Cooking time: 3 to 4 minutes

Balsamic glaze is a rich, seasoned sauce made with a reduction of good-quality balsamic vinegar. Look for it near the salad dressings and marinades in the grocery store. Since balsamic vinegar and mushrooms have a natural affinity, this is a happy marriage of flavors. Make a big batch of these unique "fries" for parties and serve them with Sicilian Meatballs (page 135) or Sweet-and-Sour Turkey Meatballs (page 111). For larger groups, simply double or triple the recipe.

Cooking spray
4 large portobello mushrooms, stems trimmed
1 tablespoon balsamic glaze or syrup
1 teaspoon dried thyme
Salt and freshly ground black pepper

Nutrients per serving:
Calories: 36
Fat: 0g
Saturated Fat: 0g
Cholesterol: 0mg
Carbohydrate: 7g
Protein: 2g
Fiber: 1g
Sodium: 7mg

Coat a stovetop grill pan or griddle with cooking spray and preheat over medium-high heat.

Cut the mushroom caps into thin strips and place in a medium bowl. Add the balsamic glaze and thyme and toss to coat.

Place the mushroom strips in the hot pan and cook for 3 to 4 minutes, turning frequently, until golden brown on all sides. Season to taste with salt and pepper.

Baked Ranch Onion Rings

Serves 4 ■ Prep time: 15 minutes ■ Cooking time: 20 minutes

These thick, golden brown rings get their stellar crunch from a coating of crushed saltine crackers, buttermilk, and Italian seasoning. The exterior bakes up golden brown and crisp while the sweet yellow onion tenderizes underneath. In our house, we like to serve the rings with loads of ketchup. For larger groups, simply double or triple the recipe.

Cooking spray
1 sleeve whole wheat saltine crackers (about 41 crackers)
1 tablespoon salt-free Italian seasoning
1½ cups low-fat buttermilk
½ cup plus 2 tablespoons all-purpose flour
¼ teaspoon ground black pepper
1 large yellow onion

Nutrients per serving:
Calories: 251
Fat: 4g
Saturated Fat: 2g
Cholesterol: 6mg
Carbohydrate: 46g
Protein: 8g
Fiber: 2g
Sodium: 575mg

Preheat the oven to 400°F. Coat a large baking sheet with cooking spray.

Combine the crackers and Italian seasoning in a food processor and process until finely ground. Transfer the mixture to a shallow bowl. Set aside.

Whisk together the buttermilk, 2 tablespoons of the flour, and the black pepper in another shallow bowl. Place the remaining ½ cup flour in a large freezer bag.

Cut the onion crosswise into ½-inch-thick slices. Separate the slices into rings (reserve and refrigerate the smaller pieces and use them in another dish). Add the onion rings to the bag with the flour and shake to coat. Working in batches, dip the flour-coated onion rings into the buttermilk mixture and then into the cracker mixture. Arrange the rings, in a single layer, on the prepared baking sheet. Bake for 20 minutes, or until the onion is tender and the coating is crisp and golden brown.

Jicama Sticks with Roasted Red Pepper Dip

Serves 4 ■ Prep time: 10 to 15 minutes

Jicama is a wonderfully crunchy vegetable that tastes like a cross between a potato and an apple. In this dish, the crunchy treat is served with a creamy roasted red pepper–spiked vegetable cream cheese. Fresh basil is added to help bring out the vegetable flavor in the cream cheese. But the best part about this side dish is that it requires no cooking, so you can whip it together in a flash.

The dip can be made up to 3 days in advance and refrigerated until ready to serve.

Nutrients per serving:

Calories: 173

Fat: 4g

Saturated Fat: 3g

Cholesterol: 13mg

Carbohydrate: 31g

Protein: 4g

Fiber: 15g

Sodium: 250mg

1 cup chopped roasted red peppers

4 ounces light vegetable cream cheese, softened

2 tablespoons chopped fresh basil

Salt and freshly ground black pepper

1 large jicama, peeled and cut into thin strips

In a food processor, combine the red peppers, cream cheese, and basil. Puree until smooth. Season to taste with salt and pepper.

Serve the dip with the jicama sticks on the side.

Butternut Squash with Maple Butter

Serves 4 ■ Prep time: 10 minutes ■ Cooking time: 1 hour

Butternut squash is already naturally sweet, but the addition of maple syrup and brown sugar makes this a sweet side dish that all kids will adore. And since butternut squash is crammed with nutrients, that's a great thing!

1 large butternut squash, halved lengthwise

Salt and freshly ground black pepper

3 tablespoons pure maple syrup

1 tablespoon unsalted butter, melted

2 teaspoons light brown sugar

½ teaspoon ground cinnamon

Nutrients per serving:

Calories: 137

Fat: 3g

Saturated Fat: 2g

Cholesterol: 8mg

Carbohydrate: 29g

Protein: 1g

Fiber: 3g

Sodium: 8mg

Preheat the oven to 400°F.

Scoop out the seeds and stringy stuff from the butternut squash halves. Using a sharp knife, score the inside of each half several times. Place the halves in a shallow baking dish, cut side up. Add about ¼ inch of water to the bottom of the baking dish to prevent the skins from burning. Season the inside of the squash with salt and pepper.

In a small bowl, whisk together the maple syrup, butter, sugar, and cinnamon. Brush the mixture inside each squash half.

Bake for 1 hour, until the squash is very soft and the tops are browned.

Grilled Honey-Lime Corn

Serves 4 ■ Prep time: 10 minutes ■ Cooking time: 6 minutes

The combination of sweet honey and tart lime really complements corn. I also add a little smoky cumin for a greater depth of flavor. For finicky eaters, though, you can leave the cumin out. For larger groups, simply double or triple the recipe.

Nutrients per serving:
Calories: 93
Fat: 1g
Saturated Fat: 0g
Cholesterol: 0mg
Carbohydrate: 23g
Protein: 2g
Fiber: 2g
Sodium: 4mg

Cooking spray
4 ears corn, shucked
Salt and freshly ground black pepper
2 tablespoons honey
Juice and zest of 1 lime
½ teaspoon ground cumin

Coat a stovetop grill pan with cooking spray and preheat over medium-high heat. Season the corn all over with salt and pepper. Place the corn in the hot pan and cook for 3 minutes, turning frequently, until golden brown on all sides.

Meanwhile, whisk together the honey, 1 tablespoon of the lime juice, 1 teaspoon of the lime zest, and the cumin. Brush the honey mixture all over the corn and cook for 2 to 3 more minutes, until the corn is tender.

Maple-Dijon Roasted Brussels Sprouts

Serves 4 ■ Prep time: 10 to 15 minutes ■ Cooking time: 15 to 18 minutes

There are three layers of coating on these sprouts: a flour base layer, a sweet maple-Dijon layer, and a golden toasted panko layer. The combination creates incredible flavor and crunch and makes this dish perfect for finicky eaters.

The Brussels sprouts can be assembled (coated) up to 24 hours in advance and refrigerated until ready to bake.

Cooking spray

2 tablespoons all-purpose flour

¼ cup panko (Japanese bread crumbs)

Salt and freshly ground black pepper

3 tablespoons pure maple syrup

2 teaspoons Dijon mustard

14 ounces thawed frozen Brussels sprouts

Preheat the oven to 375°F. Coat a large baking sheet with cooking spray.

Place the flour in a resealable plastic bag. Place the panko, ¼ teaspoon salt, and ¼ teaspoon pepper in another resealable plastic bag. In a shallow dish, whisk together the maple syrup and mustard.

Add the sprouts to the bag with the flour, seal the bag, and shake to coat. Add the flour-coated sprouts to the maple mixture and turn to coat. Transfer the sprouts to the bag with the panko, seal the bag, and shake to coat. Transfer the sprouts to the prepared baking sheet and bake for 15 to 18 minutes, until the sprouts are golden brown and tender.

Roasted Asparagus with Sun-Dried Tomato Bits

Serves 4 ■ Prep time: 10 minutes ■ Cooking time: 10 to 15 minutes

The sweetness of the sun-dried tomatoes partners perfectly with the asparagus, making this side dish excellent for finicky eaters. When roasting asparagus, it's best to work with fresh (not frozen). The cooking time will vary depending on the thickness of the spears, so start checking the oven after 10 minutes.

Cooking spray
1 pound asparagus, stem ends trimmed
Salt and freshly ground black pepper
¼ cup finely diced oil-packed sun-dried tomatoes
½ teaspoon dried oregano

Preheat the oven to 375°F. Coat a large baking sheet with cooking spray.

Arrange the asparagus on the prepared baking sheet and season to taste with salt and pepper. Sprinkle the sun-dried tomato pieces all over the asparagus. Sprinkle the oregano over the asparagus and tomato.

Roast for 10 to 15 minutes, until the asparagus is golden brown and tender.

Nutrients per serving:
Calories: 33
Fat: 1g
Saturated Fat: 0g
Cholesterol: 0mg
Carbohydrate: 5g
Protein: 2g
Fiber: 2g
Sodium: 18mg

Braised Root Vegetables with Balsamic Glaze

Serves 4 ■ Prep time: 10 minutes ■ Cooking time: 15 to 17 minutes

Braising root vegetables in a sweet and tangy glaze brings out their inherent sweetness, making this a great dish for finicky eaters. I use turnip, onion, and sweet potatoes in this dish, but you can swap ingredients in and out to suit your family. For example, use baby carrots instead of the turnip and/or red potatoes instead of the sweet potatoes.

1 tablespoon olive oil
½ cup chopped red onion
1 large turnip, peeled and chopped
1 large or 2 small sweet potatoes, peeled and chopped
⅔ cup reduced-sodium vegetable broth
¼ cup balsamic glaze or syrup
Salt and freshly ground black pepper

Heat the oil in a large skillet over medium-high heat. Add the onion and cook for 3 minutes, or until tender. Add the turnip and sweet potatoes and cook for 2 minutes, or until golden brown on all sides. Add the broth and balsamic glaze and bring to a simmer. Simmer for 10 to 12 minutes, until the vegetables are tender and the liquid has reduced and thickened. Season to taste with salt and pepper.

Parmesan-Stuffed Pretzels with Honey Mustard

Makes 16 pretzel knots ■ Prep time: 15 to 20 minutes
Cooking time: 15 to 20 minutes

These are an excellent and fun addition to any birthday party. In fact, getting the kids to help make the knots is half the fun. They can insert the cheesy "surprise" and then twist the dough into knots (or any shape they want). And, if desired, you can also serve the pretzels with warm pizza sauce on the side for dunking, instead of or in addition to the honey mustard.

The pretzels can be assembled (stuffed) up to 24 hours in advance and refrigerated until ready to bake. For larger groups, simply double or triple the recipe.

Nutrients per serving:
Calories: 112
Fat: 3g
Saturated Fat: 1g
Cholesterol: 5mg
Carbohydrate: 15g
Protein: 6g
Fiber: 1g
Sodium: 382mg

Cooking spray
1 pound frozen bread or pizza dough, thawed according to package directions
4 ounces Parmesan cheese, cut into 16 equal pieces
½ teaspoon coarse sea salt
½ cup honey mustard

Preheat the oven to 425°F. Coat a large baking sheet with cooking spray.

Separate the dough into 16 equal pieces. Roll each piece out to a ¼-inch-thick log (work on a floured surface if the dough sticks). Place one piece of the Parmesan in the center of each piece of dough. Fold the dough over to cover the cheese. Pinch the edges of the dough together to seal in the cheese. Pull the dough out far enough so you have enough to create a small knot. Tie the ends of the dough together, creating a knot. Place the knots on the prepared baking sheet, spray the knots with cooking spray, and sprinkle with the salt.

Bake for 15 to 20 minutes, until golden brown. Serve the pretzel knots with the mustard on the side.

Sweet Potato Fries with Maple-Dijon Dip

Serves 4 ■ Prep time: 10 minutes ■ Cooking time: 25 minutes

I like the combination of smoky cumin with sweet potatoes and sweet maple syrup. For finicky eaters, you can leave the cumin off some or all of the fries. You can also make the sweet yet tangy dip with low-fat Greek yogurt instead of sour cream. For larger groups, simply double or triple the recipe.

Cooking spray

2 large sweet potatoes, peeled and cut into ½-inch-thick sticks

Salt and freshly ground black pepper

1 teaspoon ground cumin

½ cup light sour cream

2 tablespoons pure maple syrup

1 teaspoon Dijon mustard

Nutrients per serving:

Calories: 151

Fat: 3g

Saturated Fat: 1.5g

Cholesterol: 10mg

Carbohydrate: 28g

Protein: 4g

Fiber: 3g

Sodium: 84mg

Preheat the oven to 400°F. Coat a large baking sheet with cooking spray.

Arrange the sweet potatoes on the prepared baking sheet and spray the surface of the potatoes with cooking spray. Season the sweet potatoes with salt and pepper. Sprinkle the cumin over the potatoes. Bake for 25 minutes, or until the sweet potatoes are golden brown and tender.

Meanwhile, in a medium bowl, whisk together the sour cream, maple syrup, and mustard. Serve the sweet potato fries with the dip on the side.

Green Apple Salad with Gorgonzola & Almonds

Serves 4 ■ Prep time: 15 minutes

The tartness of Granny Smith apples partners perfectly with sweet yet sharp blue cheese. I like to add lightly toasted almonds for their fabulous flavor and crunch. For finicky eaters, substitute diced cheddar cheese or your favorite cheese variety.

Nutrients per serving:
Calories: 152
Fat: 6g
Saturated Fat: 2g
Cholesterol: 8mg
Carbohydrate: 23g
Protein: 4g
Fiber: 3g
Sodium: 127mg

¼ cup slivered blanched almonds

2 Granny Smith apples, cored and thinly sliced (peeled if desired)

⅓ cup crumbled Gorgonzola or blue cheese

2 tablespoons honey

1 tablespoon cider vinegar

Salt and freshly ground black pepper

Place the almonds in a small dry skillet over medium heat. Cook for 3 minutes, shaking the pan frequently, until the almonds are golden brown and toasted. Remove the pan from the heat.

In a large bowl, combine the apples and cheese. In a small bowl, whisk together the honey and vinegar, then add the mixture to the apples and cheese and stir to combine. Fold in the almonds and season to taste with salt and pepper.

Celery Stalk Caesar Salad

Serves 4 ■ Prep time: 10 minutes

This fun spin on the classic Caesar salad swaps celery stalks for the traditional romaine lettuce. For a fun presentation, leave the stalks whole and serve the dressing on the side as a dip. Leave out the garlic powder if you have finicky eaters.

Nutrients per serving:
Calories: 36
Fat: 1g
Saturated Fat: <1g
Cholesterol: 2mg
Carbohydrate: 4g
Protein: 3g
Fiber: 1g
Sodium: 162mg

¾ cup reduced-sodium vegetable or chicken broth

2 tablespoons grated Parmesan cheese

1 teaspoon Dijon mustard

½ teaspoon garlic powder

4 cups chopped celery stalks

Salt and freshly ground black pepper

In a large bowl, whisk together the broth, Parmesan, mustard, and garlic powder. Add the chopped celery and toss to coat. Season to taste with salt and pepper.

Cucumber & Fresh Dill Salad

Serves 4 ■ Prep time: 10 minutes

Radishes and cucumbers are good partners, because the cucumber is mild while the radishes deliver a little kick. They come together in this dish with a blast of fresh flavor from the dill, vinegar, and honey mustard (the vinegar and honey mustard balance each other out, too). For finicky eaters, you may replace the radishes with thinly sliced beefsteak or plum tomatoes.

2 cups thinly sliced English (seedless) cucumber

½ cup thinly sliced radishes

1 tablespoon chopped fresh dill

1 tablespoon red wine vinegar

1 tablespoon olive oil

1 teaspoon honey mustard

Salt and freshly ground black pepper

Nutrients per serving:
Calories: 43
Fat: 4g
Saturated Fat: <1g
Cholesterol: 2mg
Carbohydrate: 2g
Protein: 1g
Fiber: 1g
Sodium: 17mg

In a large bowl, combine the cucumber, radishes, and dill. In a small bowl, whisk together the vinegar, oil, and mustard. Add the dressing mixture to the cucumber mixture and toss to coat. Season to taste with salt and pepper.

Asian Broccoli Slaw with Toasted Sesame Seeds

Serves 4 ■ Prep time: 10 minutes

This side dish makes an excellent addition to any party, especially because it's not your typical slaw. Broccoli is widely used in Asian dishes, so I decided to blend the distinctly Asian flavors of toasted sesame seeds, sesame oil, and soy sauce with broccoli slaw mix and red bell pepper. The salad is colorful and absolutely crammed with flavor.

The slaw can be made up to 24 hours in advance and refrigerated until ready to serve. For larger groups, simply double or triple the recipe.

2 tablespoons sesame seeds

1 (12-ounce) bag broccoli slaw (broccoli, carrots, and cabbage)

1 red bell pepper, seeded and chopped

2 tablespoons reduced-sodium soy sauce

2 teaspoons sesame oil

Salt and freshly ground black pepper

Place the sesame seeds in a small dry skillet over medium heat. Cook for 2 minutes, shaking the pan frequently, until the seeds are golden brown and toasted.

In a large bowl, combine the slaw, bell pepper, soy sauce, and sesame oil. Toss to combine. Stir in the toasted sesame seeds and season to taste with salt and pepper.

Guacamole with a Sour Cream "Spiderweb" & Blue Chips

Serves 8 ■ Prep time: 15 minutes

Nutrients per serving:
Calories: 253
Fat: 14g
Saturated Fat: 3g
Cholesterol: 5mg
Carbohydrate: 30g
Protein: 6g
Fiber: 6g
Sodium: 526mg

In this recipe, I spoon salsa between two layers of guacamole—that way, when you scoop the chips into the dip, you get a salsa surprise. And it's a great dip for parties because you can make the sour cream spiderweb into whatever shape you want (if you prefer using pastry bags, spoon the sour cream into one with a small tip and use that instead of the plastic bag). Get creative with the black olives when you make your spiders—use them whole or cut them up to make bodies and limbs; you can also use capers to make creepy, beady eyes! Make this dip finicky friendly by choosing a mild salsa and adding shredded Monterey Jack cheese.

Look for prepared guacamole in the produce section of the grocery store. I also like to order guacamole to go from my favorite Mexican restaurant (it's got a fresher taste and has little chunks of tomato, onion, and fresh cilantro in it). For larger groups, simply double or triple the recipe.

2 cups prepared guacamole
½ cup salsa of your choice
½ cup light sour cream
¼ cup pitted black olives
8 cups blue corn chips

Layer 1 cup of the guacamole in the bottom of a serving dish. Spoon the salsa over the top. Spread the remaining 1 cup guacamole over the salsa.

Spoon the sour cream into a small freezer bag and snip off one of the corners (making a hole about the size of a pencil point). Squeeze the sour cream over the guacamole, making a spiderweb design that you like. Arrange the black olives on top as spiders. Serve the chips on the side.

Spinach Salad with Honey-Bacon Dressing

Serves 4 ■ Prep time: 10 minutes

I chose a sweet and tangy honey mustard dressing for this salty and crunchy salad, but you could use a balsamic vinaigrette or ranch dressing instead. And for a wilted spinach salad, warm the dressing in the microwave for about 20 seconds before adding the bacon and dressing the spinach. For finicky eaters, you can leave out the red onion or substitute diced tomato. You can also leave out the blue cheese or substitute diced cheddar or Swiss.

Nutrients per serving:
Calories: 99
Fat: 5g
Saturated Fat: 3g
Cholesterol: 14mg
Carbohydrate: 9g
Protein: 4g
Fiber: 1g
Sodium: 390mg

4 cups baby spinach

¼ cup crumbled blue cheese

2 tablespoons minced red onion

⅓ cup light honey mustard vinaigrette or dressing

4 slices center-cut bacon, cooked until crisp and crumbled

Salt and freshly ground black pepper

In a large bowl, combine the spinach, blue cheese, and onion. In a small bowl, combine the vinaigrette and bacon. Add the dressing mixture to the spinach mixture and toss to coat. Season to taste with salt and pepper.

Cranberry Chutney with Onion & Golden Raisins

Serves 4 ■ Prep time: 15 to 20 minutes

You can serve and enjoy this unique dish plain (like a jazzed-up cranberry sauce), or serve it with pita triangles, whole grain crackers, or sesame bread sticks for dipping. It also makes a great topping for chicken, turkey, or pork.

The chutney can be made up to 3 days in advance and refrigerated until ready to serve. It may be served chilled, at room temperature, or warm (reheat in the microwave).

Nutrients per serving:
Calories: 200
Fat: 0g
Saturated Fat: 0g
Cholesterol: 0mg
Carbohydrate: 52g
Protein: 1g
Fiber: 2g
Sodium: 86mg

1 (16-ounce) can whole berry cranberry sauce
¼ cup minced white onion
¼ cup golden raisins
2 teaspoons Dijon mustard
1 teaspoon cider vinegar
Salt and freshly ground black pepper

In a medium saucepan, combine the cranberry sauce, onion, raisins, mustard, and vinegar. Mix well, set the pan over medium heat, and bring to a simmer. Simmer for 10 minutes, or until the onion is tender and the chutney is thick. Season to taste with salt and pepper. Serve warm, at room temperature, or chilled.

Pecan Tartlets

Individual Frozen Citrus Pies

Banana Ice Cream with Toasted Walnuts

Mango-Honey Sherbet with Lime

White Chocolate Truffles with Raspberry Sauce

Nutty Coffee Ice Cream with Chocolate Fudge

Slivered Almond Meringue Cookies

Chocolate Angel Food Cake

Chocolate-Coconut Pops

White Chocolate–Dipped Strawberry Screamers

Individual Strawberry Shortcakes

Crispy Sugared Wonton Ice-Cream Sandwiches

Individual Peach Cobblers

Cherry Cheesecake Pops

Grilled Banana Splits with Candied Peanuts

Pear & Cherry Cobbler

Raspberry Coulis in Meringue Cups

Individual Winter & Summer Fruit Tarts

Chocolate-Covered Kiwi Pops

Cinnamon-Sugar Baked Tortilla Chips

Ultimate Flourless Chocolate Cake

CHAPTER 7

Desserts for the Kid in You

Pecan Tartlets

Makes 12 tartlets ■ Prep time: 10 minutes ■ Cooking time: 25 to 30 minutes

Think of these as individual pecan pies. I like to serve these sweet, nutty gems with whipped cream that I've spiked with a little maple syrup or cinnamon. And for chocolate-pecan tartlets (heavenly), add ¼ cup mini semisweet chocolate morsels when you add the pecans to the egg mixture.

The tartlets can be baked up to 24 hours in advance and stored at room temperature until ready to serve. For larger groups, simply double or triple the recipe.

Nutrients per serving:
Calories: 232
Fat: 11g
Saturated Fat: 3g
Cholesterol: 33mg
Carbohydrate: 33g
Protein: 2g
Fiber: 1g
Sodium: 85mg

1 (9-inch) refrigerated piecrust
1¼ cups packed light brown sugar
2 large eggs
1 teaspoon vanilla extract
¾ cup chopped pecans

Preheat the oven to 350°F. Divide the piecrust into 12 equal pieces and press the pieces into the bottom and up the sides of a 12-cup mini muffin pan.

In a large bowl, whisk together the brown sugar, eggs, and vanilla. Fold in the pecans. Spoon the pecan mixture into the piecrusts to fill them about three-quarters full.

Bake for 25 to 30 minutes, until the filling is puffed up and the crust is lightly golden brown.

Individual Frozen Citrus Pies

Makes 8 pies ■ Prep time: 15 to 20 minutes ■ Freezing time: 1 hour

You can make these pies with any citrus juice and zest you want; orange, lime, lemon, grapefruit—they're all fabulous. And because you make them ahead and freeze them, you can pull them out of the freezer any time you want. Trust me, you'll want to keep a stash on hand so that you can satisfy sweet cravings at a moment's notice. For larger groups, simply double or triple the recipe.

16 graham cracker squares (8 rectangles)

2 tablespoons light butter or margarine, melted

1 (14-ounce) can fat-free sweetened condensed milk

Juice and zest of 2 oranges

1 (8-ounce) tub frozen light nondairy whipped topping, thawed according to package directions

Nutrients per serving:
Calories: 250
Fat: 6g
Saturated Fat: 4g
Cholesterol: 7mg
Carbohydrate: 43g
Protein: 5g
Fiber: 1g
Sodium: 169mg

Preheat the oven to 400°F.

Place the graham crackers in a food processor and process until finely ground. Add the melted butter and process until blended.

Line 8 muffin cups with paper liners. Spoon the graham cracker mixture into the bottom of each paper liner (about 1½ tablespoons per muffin cup). Press down to form a firm crust. Bake for 8 minutes, or until the crust is crisp.

Meanwhile, in a large bowl, whisk together the condensed milk, ⅓ cup of the orange juice, and 2 teaspoons of the orange zest. Fold in the whipped topping. Spoon the mixture into the prepared crusts. Freeze until firm, about 1 hour.

Banana Ice Cream with Toasted Walnuts

Serves 4 ■ Prep time: 15 minutes

In this creamy treat, sweet bananas are partnered with crunchy walnuts and dark corn syrup. The flavors envelop your palate and truly satisfy. You can also make the dessert with pecans, macadamia nuts, or hazelnuts.

You can make the ice cream up to 2 weeks in advance and freeze until ready to serve. For larger groups, simply double or triple the recipe.

½ cup walnut pieces
1 tablespoon dark corn syrup
2 very ripe bananas
2 cups light vanilla ice cream, softened
1 teaspoon vanilla extract

Nutrients per serving:
Calories: 253
Fat: 12g
Saturated Fat: 3g
Cholesterol: 18mg
Carbohydrate: 34g
Protein: 6g
Fiber: 2g
Sodium: 57mg

Place the walnuts in a small dry skillet over medium heat. Cook for 3 minutes, shaking the pan frequently, until the walnuts are golden brown and toasted. Add the corn syrup, stir to coat the walnuts, and remove from the heat.

In a large bowl, using a potato masher or fork, mash the bananas into a fine puree. Add the ice cream and vanilla and mix well. Freeze briefly to firm up, if necessary. Spoon the ice cream into bowls and top with the walnuts.

Mango-Honey Sherbet with Lime

Serves 4 ■ Prep time: 10 to 15 minutes ■ Freezing time: 1 hour

Kids will love the sweetness that mango adds to this fabulous dessert. Truth is, it also makes a healthy after-school snack. I like sherbet for birthday parties because it's nontraditional, and you can vary the flavors to coordinate with the cake just as easily as with ice cream. For example, you can make this sherbet with pineapple or strawberries instead of the mango. For larger groups, simply double or triple the recipe.

2 cups chopped mango
1 cup low-fat (1%) milk
½ cup orange juice
3 tablespoons honey
Juice and zest of 1 lime

Nutrients per serving:
Calories: 126
Fat: 1g
Saturated Fat: <1g
Cholesterol: 3mg
Carbohydrate: 29g
Protein: 3g
Fiber: 2g
Sodium: 29mg

In a food processor or blender, combine the mango, milk, orange juice, honey, 1 tablespoon of the lime juice, and ½ teaspoon of the lime zest. Puree until smooth. Transfer the mixture to a bowl or airtight container and freeze until firm, about 1 hour.

White Chocolate Truffles with Raspberry Sauce

Makes 36 truffles ■ Prep time: 15 minutes ■ Cooling time: 1 hour 30 minutes

The striking contrast of the white truffles and red raspberry sauce is a feast for the eyes as well as the palate. For a smooth raspberry sauce, strain the finished sauce through a fine-mesh sieve to remove the seeds. For larger groups, simply double or triple the recipe.

Nutrients per serving:
Calories: 104
Fat: 6g
Saturated Fat: 4g
Cholesterol: 6mg
Carbohydrate: 12g
Protein: 2g
Fiber: 1g
Sodium: 44mg

- **1¼ pounds white chocolate**
- **8 ounces light cream cheese, softened**
- **1 teaspoon vanilla extract**
- **10 ounces unsweetened thawed frozen raspberries**
- **¼ cup confectioners' sugar**

Melt 8 ounces of the chocolate in the microwave, a double boiler, or a heatproof bowl set over a saucepan of simmering water. Set aside.

Beat the cream cheese and vanilla together in a bowl until smooth and creamy. Beat in the melted chocolate. Transfer the bowl to the refrigerator and chill until firm, about 30 minutes.

Cover a baking sheet with parchment or waxed paper. Shape the cream cheese mixture into 36 balls, about 1 tablespoon of the mixture for each truffle, and transfer the balls to the prepared baking sheet.

Melt the remaining 12 ounces of chocolate in the microwave, a double boiler, or a heatproof bowl set over a saucepan of simmering water. Spear each cream cheese ball with a wooden pick or small fork and immerse the balls in the melted chocolate, turning to coat them. Return the chocolate-coated balls to the prepared baking sheet and refrigerate until firm, about 1 hour.

Meanwhile, combine the raspberries and confectioners' sugar in a small saucepan. Set the pan over medium heat and bring to a simmer. Simmer for 5 to 7 minutes, until the raspberries break down and the sauce thickens.

Serve the truffles with the raspberry sauce on the side.

Nutty Coffee Ice Cream with Chocolate Fudge

Serves 4 ■ Prep time: 15 minutes

Nutrients per serving:
Calories: 408
Fat: 23g
Saturated Fat: 13g
Cholesterol: 49mg
Carbohydrate: 46g
Protein: 6g
Fiber: 1g
Sodium: 167mg

I adore peanut brittle—both the stuff you get at a good candy store and the prepackaged brands you find at your local drugstore! For this ice cream, I break the candy into little pieces and weave it into coffee ice cream. For finicky eaters, select your favorite ice-cream flavor—chocolate and vanilla always work too!

The ice-cream mixture can be made up to 2 weeks in advance and frozen until ready to serve. For larger groups, simply double or triple the recipe.

2 cups light coffee ice cream, softened
1¼ cups crumbled peanut brittle
½ cup chocolate fudge sauce
1 cup whipped cream or whipped topping

In a large bowl, combine the ice cream and 1 cup of the peanut brittle. Mix well. Refreeze briefly to firm up.

Warm the chocolate fudge sauce in the microwave or a small saucepan over low heat. Spoon the ice-cream mixture into bowls and top with the warm fudge sauce, whipped cream, and the remaining ¼ cup peanut brittle.

Slivered Almond Meringue Cookies

Makes 36 cookies ■ Prep time: 15 minutes ■ Cooking time: 35 minutes
Cooling time: 30 minutes

Meringue cookies are light and wonderful, making them a fantastic addition to any party. This version blends the flavors of vanilla and almond in a crisp-on-the-outside, chewy-on-the-inside treat. And because they boast protein and very little fat, these are cookies you can feel good about serving. For larger groups, simply double or triple the recipe.

Nutrients per serving:
Calories: 24
Fat: <1g
Saturated Fat: 0g
Cholesterol: 0mg
Carbohydrate: 4g
Protein: 1g
Fiber: <1g
Sodium: 6mg

4 large egg whites
⅛ teaspoon cream of tartar
Pinch of salt
1 cup sugar
2 teaspoons vanilla extract
½ cup slivered blanched almonds

Preheat the oven to 250°F. Line two baking sheets with parchment paper.

With an electric mixer, beat together the egg whites, cream of tartar, and salt on low speed until the mixture is foamy. Increase the mixer speed to high and beat until soft peaks form. Gradually beat in the sugar until blended. Add the vanilla and beat until stiff peaks form and the egg whites are glossy. Fold in the almonds.

Drop the batter by scant tablespoons onto the prepared baking sheets, about 1½ inches apart. Bake for 35 minutes, rotating the pans and switching which rack they're on halfway through cooking.

Turn off the oven and let the cookies rest in the oven for 30 minutes. Remove the cookies from the oven and let cool completely at room temperature.

Chocolate Angel Food Cake

Serves 8 ■ Prep time: 10 to 15 minutes ■ Cooking time: 45 to 55 minutes
Cooling time: 15 minutes

Angel food cake is, no doubt, one of my favorite desserts. It's light and airy and even better when made with chocolate. To make sure you get the most "air" from your egg whites, start with them at room temperature (pull them from the refrigerator about 20 minutes before you begin whipping them).

The cake can be made up to 3 days in advance and stored at room temperature until ready to serve. For larger groups, simply double or triple the recipe and make two to three cakes.

Nutrients per serving:
Calories: 183
Fat: 0g
Saturated Fat: 0g
Cholesterol: 0mg
Carbohydrate: 41g
Protein: 8g
Fiber: 1g
Sodium: 144mg

1½ cups sugar
1 cup all-purpose flour
¼ cup unsweetened cocoa powder
¼ teaspoon salt
12 large egg whites, at room temperature
1 teaspoon vanilla extract

Preheat the oven to 325°F. Sift 1 cup of the sugar with the flour, cocoa powder, and salt. Combine the egg whites and vanilla in a bowl and beat with an electric mixer on medium-high speed until soft peaks form. Increase the speed to high and beat in the remaining ½ cup sugar. Beat until semistiff peaks form (do not overbeat). With a plastic spatula, gently fold in the sifted dry ingredients, ¼ cup at a time, until blended. Pour the batter into an ungreased 10-inch tube pan and spread to even out the top.

Bake for 45 to 55 minutes, until the cake springs back when touched. Invert the cake pan (turn it upside down) onto a cooling rack. Let cool for at least 15 minutes. Remove the cake gently from the pan and cut into 8 slices.

Chocolate-Coconut Pops

Makes 48 pops ■ Prep time: 20 to 25 minutes
Cooking time: 20 minutes ■ Cooling time: 10 minutes

These were my son Kyle's idea—chocolate-covered macaroon pops! I took his favorite chewy coconut macaroon cookies and dunked them in melted semisweet chocolate. Once the chocolate sets, it's bliss on a stick. (By the way, you will need 48 craft sticks for this recipe.)

The pops can be made up to 3 days in advance and stored at room temperature until ready to serve. You can also freeze the chocolate-covered pops in freezer bags for up to 3 months. At our house, we eat them straight from the freezer! For larger groups, simply double or triple the recipe.

Nutrients per serving:
Calories: 141
Fat: 8g
Saturated Fat: 7g
Cholesterol: 1mg
Carbohydrate: 17g
Protein: 2g
Fiber: 1g
Sodium: 56mg

1 (14-ounce) can fat-free sweetened condensed milk
2 large egg whites
2 teaspoons vanilla extract
⅛ teaspoon salt
2 (14-ounce) bags shredded sweetened coconut (7 cups)
2 cups semisweet chocolate morsels

Preheat the oven to 325°F. Line two large baking sheets with parchment paper.

Whisk together the condensed milk, egg whites, vanilla, and salt. Fold in the coconut until well blended. Using moistened fingers, shape the batter into 48 balls, each slightly smaller than a golf ball. Place the balls on the prepared baking sheets, about 2 inches apart.

Bake for 20 minutes, or until golden brown. Set the pans on wire racks until the balls are completely cool.

Melt the chocolate in the microwave, a double boiler, or a heatproof bowl set over a saucepan of simmering water.

Spear each ball with a craft stick. Dip the balls in the melted chocolate, turning to coat them. Return the balls to the parchment-lined baking sheets and cool completely (the chocolate will harden).

White Chocolate–Dipped Strawberry Screamers

Makes 12 strawberries ■ Prep time: 30 minutes

Make these fun faces with your kids—the expressions can be anything you want them to be, and the green strawberry tops make for perfect spiky hair. Not just for Halloween, these are a great addition to any party or get-together.

The strawberries can be made up to 3 days in advance and refrigerated until ready to serve. For larger groups, simply double or triple the recipe.

1 cup white chocolate morsels
12 large fresh strawberries with green tops intact
½ cup semisweet chocolate morsels

Coat a large baking sheet with parchment paper.

Melt the white chocolate in the microwave, a double boiler, or a heatproof bowl set over a saucepan of simmering water.

Dip the strawberries into the white chocolate, coating each berry all the way up to the stem end.

Transfer the strawberries to the parchment paper to cool. When the white chocolate is hard, melt the semisweet chocolate in the microwave, a double boiler, or a heatproof bowl set over a saucepan of simmering water.

Transfer the semisweet chocolate to a pastry bag or plastic freezer bag. Snip off one of the corners (making a hole about the size of a pencil point). Squeeze the chocolate through the corner of the bag and draw faces on the strawberries—two eyes, a mouth (and a nose if you want)! Let the semisweet chocolate set before serving.

Individual Strawberry Shortcakes

Makes 10 shortcakes ■ Prep time: 20 minutes

These shortcakes are incredibly easy to prepare thanks to a little help from prepared buttermilk biscuits. For a fancy presentation, dust the top of the assembled shortcakes with confectioners' sugar (sift the sugar through a fine-mesh sieve). And you can make the dessert finicky friendly by using your favorite berry variety or fresh or thawed frozen sliced peaches. For larger groups, simply double or triple the recipe.

Nutrients per serving:
Calories: 146
Fat: 6g
Saturated Fat: 2g
Cholesterol: 8mg
Carbohydrate: 20g
Protein: 2g
Fiber: 1g
Sodium: 361mg

Cooking spray (preferably butter flavored)
1 (12-ounce) can refrigerated buttermilk biscuits (10 biscuits)
1 tablespoon sugar
2½ cups sliced fresh strawberries
2 tablespoons orange juice
1 cup whipped cream or whipped topping

Preheat the oven to 375°F. Coat a large baking sheet with cooking spray.

Remove the biscuit dough from the can, separate the dough into 10 individual biscuits, and transfer them to the prepared baking sheet. Spray the surface of the biscuits with the cooking spray and sprinkle the sugar over the top. Bake for 8 to 10 minutes, until the biscuits are golden brown.

Meanwhile, in a medium bowl, combine the strawberries and orange juice.

Split the biscuits in half crosswise and arrange the bottom halves on plates. Spoon the strawberry mixture onto the biscuits. Arrange the top halves of the biscuits on the strawberries and spoon a dollop of whipped cream on top.

Crispy Sugared Wonton Ice-Cream Sandwiches

Makes 8 ice-cream sandwiches ■ Prep time: 25 minutes

Why relegate wonton skins to savory meals? They bake up crisp and golden brown, making them perfect for filling with sweet ice cream. For added flair, once the ice-cream sandwiches are assembled, press toasted coconut or mini chocolate morsels into the ice cream around the edges. And you can also add a little cinnamon to the sugar before sprinkling the top of the wonton sandwiches. For a chocolate version, sift sweetened cocoa powder over the ice-cream sandwiches instead of confectioners' sugar. For finicky eaters, choose your favorite ice-cream variety.

The wontons can be baked up to 24 hours in advance and stored at room temperature until ready to assemble the ice-cream sandwiches. The ice-cream sandwiches can be assembled up to 1 week in advance and frozen until ready to serve.

> **Cooking spray (preferably butter flavored)**
> **16 wonton wrappers**
> **1 tablespoon granulated sugar**
> **2 cups light Neapolitan ice cream (vanilla, chocolate, and strawberry), softened**
> **1 tablespoon confectioners' sugar**

Preheat the oven to 300°F. Coat a large baking sheet with cooking spray.

Arrange the wonton wrappers on the prepared baking sheet. Spray the surface of the wontons with the cooking spray and sprinkle the granulated sugar over the top. Bake for 6 to 8 minutes, until the wontons are golden brown. Let cool slightly.

Spoon the ice cream onto 8 of the toasted wontons. Arrange the remaining 8 wontons over the ice cream, making sandwiches. Sift the confectioners' sugar over the top and serve or freeze until ready to serve.

Individual Peach Cobblers

Makes 10 cobblers ■ Prep time: 10 to 15 minutes ■ Cooking time: 8 to 10 minutes

These individual cobblers boast cinnamon-spiked peaches nestled under tender, sugar-topped buttermilk biscuits. Once baked, the peaches are warm and wonderful and the biscuits are golden brown and sweet. For finicky eaters, substitute any fruit variety for the peaches. Sliced pears (canned in 100 percent juice), raspberries, and blueberries all work very well.

The cobblers can be assembled up to 24 hours in advance and refrigerated until ready to bake.

2½ cups fresh or thawed frozen sliced, peeled peaches
2 tablespoons confectioners' sugar
½ teaspoon ground cinnamon
1 (12-ounce) can refrigerated buttermilk biscuits (10 biscuits)
Cooking spray (preferably butter flavored)
1 tablespoon granulated sugar

Preheat the oven to 375°F.

In a large bowl, combine the peaches, confectioners' sugar, and cinnamon. Mix well. Spoon the mixture into 10 individual ovenproof ramekins.

Remove the biscuit dough from the can, separate the dough into 10 individual biscuits, and place the biscuits on top of the peaches. Spray the surface of the biscuits with the cooking spray and sprinkle the granulated sugar over the top. Bake for 8 to 10 minutes, until the biscuits are golden brown.

FLOUR

Cherry Cheesecake Pops

Makes 8 pops ■ Prep time: 10 minutes ■ Freezing time: 1 hour

Fun, creamy, and riddled with cherries: Here's a crazy-easy dessert that's truly unique. Cherry pie filling, confectioners' sugar, and vanilla are woven into cream cheese and frozen into pops. You can also make the dish with blueberry or pumpkin pie filling. For a decadent treat, dip the frozen pops into melted semisweet chocolate and freeze until the chocolate is firm. And if you don't have ice-pop molds, pour the mixture into small plastic cups, insert craft sticks, and freeze until firm.

The pops can be made up to 1 week in advance and frozen until ready to serve.

Nutrients per serving:
Calories: 127
Fat: 4g
Saturated Fat: 3g
Cholesterol: 13mg
Carbohydrate: 20g
Protein: 3g
Fiber: <1g
Sodium: 143mg

1 (16-ounce) can cherry pie filling
8 ounces light cream cheese, softened
2 tablespoons confectioners' sugar
1 teaspoon vanilla extract

In a large bowl, combine the pie filling, cream cheese, confectioners' sugar, and vanilla. Mix well. Spoon the mixture into eight ice-pop molds. Freeze until firm, about 1 hour.

Grilled Banana Splits with Candied Peanuts

Serves 4 ■ Prep time: 10 to 15 minutes

Banana splits are perfect for parties because adults and kids alike can create their own masterpieces with a variety of toppings. In this recipe, I top the decadent dessert with brown sugar–coated peanuts. I also suggest you offer colored sprinkles, caramel sauce, fudge sauce or chocolate syrup, small assorted candy pieces, and maraschino cherries. And when you halve and grill the bananas with the skin on one side, it prevents them from falling apart (making your life much easier). For larger groups, simply double or triple the recipe.

Nutrients per serving:
Calories: 364
Fat: 13g
Saturated Fat: 6g
Cholesterol: 38mg
Carbohydrate: 57g
Protein: 7g
Fiber: 4g
Sodium: 150mg

⅓ **cup dry-roasted, salted peanuts**
1 tablespoon light brown sugar
Cooking spray
4 medium bananas (preferably slightly underripe)
2 cups light ice cream of your choice
1 cup whipped cream or whipped topping

Combine the peanuts and brown sugar in a large skillet over medium heat. Cook for 3 to 5 minutes, stirring frequently, until the brown sugar melts and coats the peanuts. Remove the pan from the heat.

Coat a stovetop grill pan with cooking spray and preheat over medium-high heat. Leaving the skin on the bananas, cut them in half lengthwise. Place the bananas cut side down in the hot pan. Grill for 30 seconds to 1 minute, until the flesh is golden brown. Peel the bananas and transfer them to dessert plates.

Top the bananas with the ice cream, peanuts, and whipped cream.

Pear & Cherry Cobbler

Serves 10 ■ Prep time: 15 minutes ■ Cooking time: 8 to 10 minutes

I love the chewiness of the dried cherries with the tender pears in this comforting classic. You may substitute dried cranberries for the cherries, if desired.

The cobbler can be assembled up to 24 hours in advance and refrigerated until ready to bake. For larger groups, simply double or triple the recipe.

3 (14-ounce) cans pear halves in 100% juice, drained and diced
1 cup sweetened dried cherries
2 tablespoons cornstarch
1 (12-ounce) can refrigerated buttermilk biscuits (10 biscuits)
Cooking spray (preferably butter flavored)
1 tablespoon sugar

Preheat the oven to 375°F.

In a large bowl, combine the pears, cherries, and cornstarch. Mix well. Spoon the mixture into a shallow baking dish (about 11 by 7 inches).

Remove the biscuit dough from the can, separate the dough into 20 small pieces, and arrange the pieces on top of the pear mixture. Spray the surface of the biscuits with the cooking spray and sprinkle the sugar over the top. Bake for 8 to 10 minutes, until the biscuit topping is golden brown.

Nutrients per serving:
Calories: 213
Fat: 5g
Saturated Fat: 1g
Cholesterol: 0mg
Carbohydrate: 40g
Protein: 3g
Fiber: 3g
Sodium: 367mg

Raspberry Coulis in Meringue Cups

Makes 12 meringue cups ■ Prep time: 15 minutes
Cooking time: 35 minutes ■ Cooling time: 30 minutes

For this recipe, I decided to adapt my famous vanilla-spiked meringue cookie recipe to make little baked bowls that I could fill with fruit. What a pretty and unbelievably yummy creation! The cookies are crisp yet chewy and make the ideal bowls for the sweet raspberry puree. For finicky eaters, fill the meringue cups with anything you want, like mandarin oranges, fresh berries, ice cream, chocolate chips—you name it. Kids also love filling the cups themselves with selections from a fillings buffet. For larger groups, simply double or triple the recipe.

The meringue cups can be baked up to 24 hours in advance and stored at room temperature until ready to fill and serve.

4 large egg whites

⅛ teaspoon cream of tartar

Pinch of salt

1 cup sugar

1 teaspoon vanilla extract

1 (10-ounce) bag unsweetened frozen raspberries

Preheat the oven to 250°F. Line two baking sheets with parchment paper.

With an electric mixer, beat together the egg whites, cream of tartar, and salt on low speed until the mixture is foamy. Increase the mixer speed to high and beat until soft peaks form. Gradually beat in the sugar until blended. Add the vanilla and beat until stiff peaks form and the egg whites are glossy.

Spoon the batter onto the prepared baking sheets, making 12 mounds about 1½ inches apart. Using a spoon, press into the center of the mounds to make shallow bowls.

Bake for 35 minutes, rotating the pans and switching which rack they're on halfway through cooking. Turn off the oven and let the meringue cups rest in the oven for 30 minutes. Remove the meringue cups from the oven and let cool completely at room temperature.

Meanwhile, place the frozen raspberries in a medium saucepan over medium heat. Bring to a simmer. Simmer for 5 minutes, or until the raspberries break down. Strain the raspberries through a fine-mesh sieve to remove the seeds. Let cool at room temperature or in the refrigerator.

Spoon the raspberry coulis into the meringue cups just before serving.

Individual Winter & Summer Fruit Tarts

Makes 8 tarts ■ Prep time: 10 to 15 minutes ■ Cooking time: 25 to 30 minutes

I call these Winter & Summer Fruit Tarts because you can fill the tarts with any fruit that's in season (you can even use canned pie filling). The recipe here is a winter version because I call for apples and cinnamon. I like to use McIntosh apples in my pies and tarts because they have what seems to me the perfect balance of sweet and tart flavors. You may use your favorite apple variety (or you can use pears). For parties, ask the kids to choose their fillings and make custom tarts for everyone. For larger groups, simply double or triple the recipe.

For Summer Fruit Tarts, use peaches, nectarines, plums, or fresh berries (any variety of berry or a combination of varieties).

The tarts can be baked up to 24 hours in advance and stored at room temperature until ready to serve.

Nutrients per serving:
Calories: 152
Fat: 7g
Saturated Fat: 3g
Cholesterol: 5mg
Carbohydrate: 22g
Protein: 1g
Fiber: 1g
Sodium: 100mg

1 (9-inch) refrigerated piecrust

2 cups peeled, cored, and diced McIntosh apples

3 tablespoons sugar

1 tablespoon cornstarch

½ teaspoon ground cinnamon

Preheat the oven to 375°F. Divide the piecrust into 8 equal pieces and press the pieces into the bottom and up the sides of 8 cups in a muffin pan.

In a large bowl, combine the apples, sugar, cornstarch, and cinnamon. Mix well. Spoon the apple mixture into the piecrusts to fill them about three-quarters full.

Bake for 25 to 30 minutes, until the apples are tender and the crust is golden brown.

Chocolate-Covered Kiwi Pops

Makes 4 popsicles ■ Prep time: 20 minutes ■ Cooling time: 30 minutes

As if kiwi weren't sweet enough, I decided to dunk the fabulous fruit in a rich chocolate ganache (melted chocolate and heavy cream) before rolling it in chocolate sprinkles. The ganache is soft and melts in your mouth just as you get to the kiwi inside. For finicky eaters, you may make these pops with halved bananas or large pineapple or mango chunks. You can also dip the chocolate-coated kiwi into colored sprinkles, chopped hazelnuts, or shredded coconut. For larger groups, simply double or triple the recipe.

⅔ **cup semisweet chocolate chips**
2 tablespoons heavy cream
2 kiwis, peeled and halved lengthwise
¼ **cup chocolate sprinkles**

Line a large baking sheet with parchment paper.

Melt the chocolate in the microwave, a double boiler, or a heatproof bowl set over a saucepan of simmering water. Remove the pan from the heat, stir in the heavy cream, and mix well.

Spear each kiwi half with a craft stick. Dip the kiwi in the melted chocolate mixture, turning to coat. Roll the kiwi in the sprinkles, turning to coat all sides. Transfer the kiwi pops to the parchment-lined baking sheet and cool completely (the chocolate will harden), about 30 minutes.

Cinnamon-Sugar Baked Tortilla Chips

Serves 4 ■ Prep time: 10 to 15 minutes ■ Cooking time: 8 to 10 minutes

These chips boast an intriguing flavor combination: crispy corn chips with sweet sugar and warming cinnamon. I often nestle them into a scoop of vanilla ice cream or frozen yogurt.

The chips can be made up to 3 days in advance and stored in an airtight container at room temperature until ready to serve. For larger groups, simply double or triple the recipe.

Nutrients per serving:
Calories: 127
Fat: 1g
Saturated Fat: 0g
Cholesterol: 0mg
Carbohydrate: 28g
Protein: 3g
Fiber: 3g
Sodium: 6mg

Cooking spray (preferably butter flavored)
8 (6-inch) corn tortillas, cut into 8 wedges each
1½ to 2 tablespoons sugar
½ teaspoon ground cinnamon

Preheat the oven to 400°F. Coat a large baking sheet with cooking spray.

Arrange the tortillas on the prepared baking sheet and spray the surface of the tortillas with cooking spray. Sprinkle the sugar and cinnamon over the tortillas.

Bake for 8 to 10 minutes, until the tortilla chips are golden brown and crispy.

Ultimate Flourless Chocolate Cake

Serves 8 ■ Prep time: 15 minutes ■ Cooking time: 25 minutes
Cooling time: 5 minutes

Nutrients per serving:
Calories: 231
Fat: 15g
Saturated Fat: 8g
Cholesterol: 81mg
Carbohydrate: 25g
Protein: 5g
Fiber: 2g
Sodium: 91mg

If this book had an "amazing" icon, it would be stamped all over this page. Trust me: This cake is sinful and rich and downright awesome. We like very dark chocolate in our house, so I use bittersweet chocolate in this cake. You may substitute semisweet chocolate if that's your favorite.

The cake can be made up to 3 days in advance and refrigerated until ready to serve. For larger groups, simply double or triple the recipe and make two to three cakes.

Cooking spray (preferably butter flavored)
4 ounces bittersweet chocolate, chopped into small pieces
½ cup (1 stick) light butter or margarine
¾ cup sugar
3 large eggs, lightly beaten
½ cup plus 1 tablespoon unsweetened cocoa powder
¼ teaspoon salt

Preheat the oven to 375°F. Coat a 9-inch round baking pan with cooking spray. Line the pan with waxed paper and spray the waxed paper with cooking spray.

Melt the chocolate and butter together in the microwave, a double boiler, or a heatproof bowl set over a saucepan of simmering water, stirring frequently. When the mixture is smooth, remove from the heat and whisk in the sugar. Then whisk in the eggs. Sift ½ cup of the cocoa powder and the salt into the chocolate mixture and whisk until just combined.

Pour the batter into the prepared pan and bake for 25 minutes, or until the top has formed a thin crust. Set the cake in the pan on a wire rack to cool for 5 minutes. Invert the cake over a serving plate to remove from the pan, and sift the remaining 1 tablespoon cocoa powder over the top.

Metric Conversions and Equivalents

METRIC CONVERSION FORMULAS

TO CONVERT	MULTIPLY
Ounces to grams	Ounces by 28.35
Pounds to kilograms	Pounds by .454
Teaspoons to milliliters	Teaspoons by 4.93
Tablespoons to milliliters	Tablespoons by 14.79
Fluid ounces to milliliters	Fluid ounces by 29.57
Cups to milliliters	Cups by 236.59
Cups to liters	Cups by .236
Pints to liters	Pints by .473
Quarts to liters	Quarts by .946
Gallons to liters	Gallons by 3.785
Inches to centimeters	Inches by 2.54

APPROXIMATE METRIC EQUIVALENTS

VOLUME

¼ teaspoon	1 milliliter
½ teaspoon	2.5 milliliters
¾ teaspoon	4 milliliters
1 teaspoon	5 milliliters
1¼ teaspoons	6 milliliters
1½ teaspoons	7.5 milliliters
1¾ teaspoons	8.5 milliliters
2 teaspoons	10 milliliters
1 tablespoon (½ fluid ounce)	15 milliliters
2 tablespoons (1 fluid ounce)	30 milliliters
¼ cup	60 milliliters
⅓ cup	80 milliliters
½ cup (4 fluid ounces)	120 milliliters
⅔ cup	160 milliliters
¾ cup	180 milliliters
1 cup (8 fluid ounces)	240 milliliters
1¼ cups	300 milliliters
1½ cups (12 fluid ounces)	360 milliliters
1⅔ cups	400 milliliters
2 cups (1 pint)	460 milliliters
3 cups	700 milliliters
4 cups (1 quart)	0.95 liter
1 quart plus ¼ cup	1 liter
4 quarts (1 gallon)	3.8 liters

WEIGHT

¼ ounce	7 grams
½ ounce	14 grams
¾ ounce	21 grams
1 ounce	28 grams
1¼ ounces	35 grams
1½ ounces	42.5 grams
1⅔ ounces	45 grams
2 ounces	57 grams
3 ounces	85 grams
4 ounces (¼ pound)	113 grams
5 ounces	142 grams
6 ounces	170 grams
7 ounces	198 grams
8 ounces (½ pound)	227 grams
16 ounces (1 pound)	454 grams
35.25 ounces (2.2 pounds)	1 kilogram

LENGTH

⅛ inch	3 millimeters
¼ inch	6 millimeters
½ inch	1¼ centimeters
1 inch	2½ centimeters
2 inches	5 centimeters
2½ inches	6 centimeters
4 inches	10 centimeters
5 inches	13 centimeters
6 inches	15¼ centimeters
12 inches (1 foot)	30 centimeters

OVEN TEMPERATURES

To convert Fahrenheit to Celsius, subtract 32 from Fahrenheit, multiply the result by 5, then divide by 9.

DESCRIPTION	FAHRENHEIT	CELSIUS	BRITISH GAS MARK
Very cool	200°	95°	0
Very cool	225°	110°	¼
Very cool	250°	120°	½
Cool	275°	135°	1
Cool	300°	150°	2
Warm	325°	165°	3
Moderate	350°	175°	4
Moderately hot	375°	190°	5
Fairly hot	400°	200°	6
Hot	425°	220°	7
Very hot	450°	230°	8
Very hot	475°	245°	9

COMMON INGREDIENTS AND THEIR APPROXIMATE EQUIVALENTS

1 cup uncooked white rice = 185 grams

1 cup all-purpose flour = 140 grams

1 stick butter (4 ounces • ½ cup • 8 tablespoons) = 110 grams

1 cup butter (8 ounces • 2 sticks • 16 tablespoons) = 220 grams

1 cup brown sugar, firmly packed = 225 grams

1 cup granulated sugar = 200 grams

Information compiled from a variety of sources, including *Recipes into Type* by Joan Whitman and Dolores Simon (Newton, MA: Biscuit Books, 2000); *The New Food Lover's Companion* by Sharon Tyler Herbst (Hauppauge, NY: Barron's, 1995); and *Rosemary Brown's Big Kitchen Instruction Book* (Kansas City, MO: Andrews McMeel, 1998).

Index